What Others Are Saying...

DAWN FORD:
"If you're looking for that one book that covers everything about raising your dog to be well trained, I personally don't believe there's a book out there that delivers more value than Michele Welton's vocabulary program."

CONNIE HILLER:
"No dog owner can afford to be without this book. It is the most sensible teaching program I've ever read. The lessons are easy to understand and easy to follow."

JASON RICHARDSON:
"Buy it, you'll love it! The best dog-raising book I've ever read, bar none!"

RHONDA SACOWICZ:
"Michele, I love the way you write. Super book, I highly recommend it to anyone who wants a smarter dog."

CHRIS GONZALES:
"I can't thank you enough for this terrific book. It's like a gold mine. It explains everything you need to know to get your dog acting like a gentleman."

JOSEPH ADINARO:
"This book tells you not only what does work, but what doesn't. Before I bought your book I was doing a lot of the 'doesn't work' and it showed in my Dobermann's stubborn behavior. Now I'm doing what you tell me 'does work' and his stubbornness is completely gone."

DENNIS APPLEBERRY:
"In my humble opinion, this is the most practical course on family dog training you will find anywhere. Whatever your dog needs to know, it's in this book."

KELLY AUSTIN:
"I have an Australian Shepherd that I've allowed to not respect me. I've changed my ways in the last few days and she's responding much better. Thank you again!"

SHOMIR BANERJEE:
"Your book is simply amazing. It went far beyond my expectations. I believe it is going to be the single best investment I have ever made, when it comes to my dog."

JANET CARROLL:
"We have a 16 week old Wheaten Terrier. She is definitely smart but does want to 'sass' me occasionally. I have been working with her on this rude behavior and within one day using some of the techniques you have suggested, she is much better! All this to say, your book is great! It totally makes sense to teach my dog 100 words!"

CARLY CRIXELL:
"Just letting you know that I've learned so much from your books. In less than a month, I kid you not, Nico was a perfect dog. Your *Teach Your Dog* book completely turned him around."

PAIGE DRAGICH:
"I want to tell you that I have gotten at least 50 times the value out of your book compared to what I paid for it. Your educational programs work like a charm. I'm so happy with my dog now."

TERRY HALE

"I'm really enjoying your *100 Words*…have learned a lot about how to be a proactive 'parent' to our newest family member, a rescued six month old Basset, Simon. Thanks so much for your delightful writing style and immense amount of information."

MARCIA DUCHARME:

"I learned how to communicate with my dog and get him to understand me and do what I say. This book makes so much sense. I like the step by step lessons."

MICHELLE FARRUNI:

"This is fun! After just a couple of days following your instructions, I can now "send" my two dogs all over my house—"Go stairs!" "Go bed!" "Go crate!" and they race each other to be the first to get there. My husband can't believe they learned this so quickly."

BRIAN FORD:

"I learned so much from your book. It's a lot deeper than just training a pup 100 words. It makes you look at other dogs and owners and gives you a better outlook on the dog world. You hit all aspects of training. A lot of folks don't seem to cover the 'What ifs' of puppy training and hit them all. You're the best!"

JEAN GOBEIL:

"I have read so many books trying to figure out how to get my dog to listen to me. I should have just bought yours first. All I had to do was follow your plan and everything worked just like you said. Tiki behaves so much better now, I just love it!"

LAURA MARTEL:

"What an excellent course you developed. I was surprised at the detail you go into. Your book is one of the few that really lives up to the promises made. Great stuff!"

DIANNA MILLS:

"This book told me everything I needed to do to make Shadow a better family dog. That's what I wanted and that's exactly what I have now, after reading your book and following your advice. It worked!"

SUE MUNDY:

"We got this book just in time. I was about to spoil a perfectly good Yorkshire Terrier. Thank you so much for your wonderful, straightforward advice."

ANDREW RIGATTO:

"I am completely blown away by your vocabulary and respect program. You've pulled everything together into one solid package of sensible dog training. Anyone can follow this program, no experience needed, and end up with a much better dog."

SCOTT STINGLEY:

"Even if you're just thinking of getting a puppy, you should definitely buy this manual. The time and effort you put into reading it will put you way ahead of most puppy owners and save you months of trial and error and searching for answers. Trust me, the answers are all here in this book!"

LEE YEAGER:

"Michele, I feel like I already know you, from the friendly way you write. Your book and advice has made a world of difference in our dog's behavior and I just wanted to say thanks."

Teach Your Dog
100 English Words

The A+
Dog Training Program
For Good Manners
and Happy Obedience

Michele Welton

Petbridge LLC—Yellow Springs, Ohio

Teach Your Dog 100 English Words, by Michele Welton

Copyright © 2010 Michele Welton. All rights reserved.

Published by Petbridge LLC, Yellow Springs, OH, www.petbridge.com

Petbridge LLC is minimizing its impact on the environment and helping safe-guard the world's ancient and endangered forests by printing on FSC-certified cover stock and FSC-certified, acid-free paper.
Printed in the United States of America.

Cover design by Di Natale Design, www.dinataledesign.com
Interior design by 1106 Design, www.1106design.com

Disclaimer
This book is intended to provide general information about dog training. It should not be used as your sole source of information for training your dog, as the advice contained herein may not be applicable to your particular dog. The author and publisher make no representations or warranties about the accuracy, applicability, or completeness of the information in this book, and assume no liability for any consequences, loss, or damage caused or alleged to be caused by the information in this book.

ISBN: 978-0-9797091-0-4 (Softcover)
Library of Congress Control Number: 2009901953

About the Author

Hello! I'm Michele Welton and I've been involved with dogs for over 35 years. That's my husband and me in the photo, with our Miniature Poodle, Buffy (The Vampire Slayer).

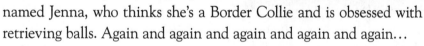

We also have a Chihuahua named Mouse, who came to live with us when she was diagnosed with liver cancer. Happily, her cancer is now in remission.

Plus an energetic young Papillon named Jenna, who thinks she's a Border Collie and is obsessed with retrieving balls. Again and again and again and again and again...

Lest you think I know only about small breeds, the first three loves of my life were German Shepherds, and I've trained and shown many breeds, crossbreeds, and mixed breeds in competitive canine events such as obedience, agility, herding, tracking, and schutzhund.

So, for over 35 years, I've been one or more of the following: dog lover, owner, trainer, competitor, obedience instructor, behavioral consultant, breed selection consultant, and author of more than a dozen books on choosing, raising, and training dogs.

I'm pleased to meet a fellow dog lover! Enjoy the book, and when you're done reading, please visit my web site at *www.yourpurebredpuppy.com*.

More Books by Michele Welton

Dog Care Wisdom: 11 Things You Must Do Right To Keep Your Dog Healthy and Happy.
Learn how to raise your dog in all the right ways to avoid health problems and maximize his chances of living a long, healthy, comfortable life.

How To Buy a Good Dog
Read this book BEFORE you get a dog. You'll learn how to choose the right kind of dog, find the right breeder or animal shelter or rescue group, and select the right individual puppy or adult dog—one who will grow up to be smart, good-natured, and healthy.

Test Your Dog's IQ
These 25 IQ tests will measure your dog's problem-solving abilities, memory, and observation skills. They're challenging for your dog— and fun for both of you. You may want to videotape your dog taking these tests!

These and other dog books are available
from the author's website:
www.yourpurebredpuppy.com

Table of Contents

List of Vocabulary Words

Chapter 1

How to Ruin a Perfectly Good Pet

Consider these three philosophies:

- "Dogs should not be restricted by rules and expectations."
- "Dogs should be completely uninhibited."
- "I just want my dog to be my friend."

If you want to raise a well-behaved dog, these three philosophies don't work. Oh, you'll end up with an unrestricted, uninhibited dog, all right, but he will also be uneducated, unruly, unreliable, and ultimately unhappy. Both of you, in fact, will be unhappy.

Keep reading and you'll learn why an uneducated, unrestricted dog is not a happy camper!

Is your dog rude?

I often get phone calls from distressed owners who are having trouble with their dog. Let's listen in on a phone conversation between myself and a typical dog owner.

We're about to meet Kathy Armstrong and Jake—a well-meaning owner and her good-natured but undisciplined dog, both of whom will follow us through this book.

Kathy: "Michele, my dog Jake is being difficult. I can't make him do anything. He only listens to me when he's in the mood."

Michele: "I see. Would you say Jake is behaving rudely?"

Kathy (surprised): "What do you mean? How can a dog be rude?"

Ah, how indeed? Let us count the ways!

Talking back
Michele: "Does Jake sass you when you tell him to do something? Does he bark back at you?"

Kathy: "Well, yes, if he doesn't want to do something."

Staying just out of your reach
Michele: "When you reach your hand toward him, does he often dart away from you, just out of reach?"

Kathy: "Well, yes, if he doesn't want to be caught."

Hanging onto objects
Michele: "Does he brace his legs and refuse to let go when you try to take something away from him?"

Kathy: "Yes, if it's something he wants to keep for himself."

Pestering you

Michele: "Does he persistently nudge or pester you for attention when you're trying to read the newspaper or when you talk on the phone or visit with guests?"

Kathy: "Yes, when I'm not paying attention to him."

Stealing food

Michele: "Does he steal food off your plate when you leave it unattended? Does he get into the trash?"

Kathy: "Um…"

Grumbling when annoyed

Michele: "Does he ever grumble at you when you wake him up? Or when you try to move him off his favorite chair? Or when you reach toward his food bowl while he's eating? Or when you touch some sensitive part of his body, like his tail or stomach or paw?"

Kathy: "Yes, he does growl sometimes."

Struggling during grooming

Michele: "Does he fuss when you try to open his mouth to look at his teeth? How about cleaning his ears? Or clipping his toenails?"

Kathy: "True. He doesn't like me to do those things."

Running away from you

Michele: "When you catch him doing something wrong, does he run from you? Does he lead you on a merry chase around the house or yard?"

Kathy: "Uh-huh. So he can't be scolded."

"Getting back at you"

Michele: "When he doesn't get his own way or when he's upset with you, does he ever chew things or pee somewhere in the house?"

Kathy: "Yup! I think he does that to get back at me."

"Telling off" guests

Michele: "Does Jake decide who's welcome in your home and who isn't? Does he bark or grumble at visitors even after you've let them in?"

Kathy: "Well, if he's excited or if he doesn't like them…"

Jumping on guests

Michele: "Ah, and if he does like them, is he calm and polite? Or does he jump all over them?"

Silence. Then… "I'm beginning to see your point."

Michele: "And you said he only obeys when he's in the mood."

Kathy (sighing): "You're right, Michele. Jake does do quite a few of those things. But are they really that bad?"

Why rude behaviors are bad

Michele: "I'm afraid so. Those behaviors are rude and disrespectful. If a dog is allowed to do things that are rude and disrespectful, he starts believing that he is higher in the **pack order** than you are."

Kathy (puzzled): "And the pack order is…?"

Michele: "You might also call it a **pecking order**. It's like a ladder. A ladder of hierarchy. Dogs are sociable animals who like to live with other sociable animals in a group or pack. All packs have a pecking order. At the top is the most dominant animal, the **Pack Leader**. He or she establishes the rules and makes the decisions for the group.

Next in line is the Number Two animal, who can tell everyone else (except for the Pack Leader), what to do. Then the Number Three animal, and so on, right down to the most submissive one of all, who can't tell anybody else what to do.

Now you might think this kind of structure sounds harsh, but pack animals love it! They know instinctively that the well-being of the group depends upon each member being able to handle his or her respective position. With a pecking order, they know exactly where they stand with each other. They know who is who in the pack.

The pack instinct is built into your dog's genes, and it's a good thing, too, because it's why dogs wedge themselves so tightly into our families, rather than prowling along the fringes, like many cats do.

Cats tend to be more solitary animals who like to do their own thing. Dogs are pack animals who like to belong. That one instinct makes a big difference in the way each pet should be raised.

 When a dog joins your family, even if your family consists only of a single person—YOU—a pack is formed.

Oh, yes, in his mind it certainly is, and his instincts compel him to seek out its structure. His two major questions are:

Who is the leader? Who is the follower?

**Whoever is allowed to establish the rules
and make the decisions is the leader.**

If you don't establish yourself as the leader, your dog will be compelled by his instincts to assume that role. And now you will see those "rude and disrespectful" behaviors. Your dog isn't really being rude or disrespectful. He is simply carrying out his role as pack leader. Since you haven't assumed the role, he has to do it."

Kathy (anxiously): "But I don't want to rule or control my dog. I just want him to be my friend."

Michele: "Kathy, Jake can never be just your friend, because friends are equals. Jake is your **dependent**. He depends on you for his food, his health, his safety, his very life. There are times when you need to do things with Jake that he doesn't understand and doesn't like. You might need to:

- give medicine that tastes awful
- take something dangerous out of his mouth
- roll him onto his back and remove a tick from his belly

Jake doesn't understand that medicines will help him, that some things he puts in his mouth will poison him or choke him, that ticks carry disease. Without this knowledge, Jake doesn't know what's best for him. For his own safety, he has to accept YOUR greater knowledge and judgment.

> For your own peace of mind as your dog's guardian and caregiver, you must feel confident that you can restrain and handle him in any way you see fit, at any time you see fit.

But if your dog won't even accept minor things like clipping his toenails or cleaning his teeth or giving up a toy or sitting quietly while you attach his leash, then he's certainly not going to accept something major that you might need to do with him to protect him or save his life.

You simply cannot take proper care of a dog if he doesn't acknowledge you as his pack leader."

Kathy: "But I'm worried that if I take charge all the time, he'll resent me!"

Michele: "No, he won't resent you. He'll RESPECT you, and when your dog respects you, he will not only behave beautifully, but also he will feel happy and secure. Isn't that what you want for Jake?"

Kathy: "Yes!"

Chapter 2

How to Raise Your Dog to Be Smart, Happy, and Well-Behaved

In a nutshell, if you want your dog to be smart, happy, and well-behaved, he has to be a FOLLOWER—not a leader.

Why follower dogs are so happy and bright

Follower dogs are happier because they're secure

Follower dogs know you have everything under control, so they don't need to worry about trying to figure out our complicated human world. They can relax and enjoy life while you handle all the decisions.

Follower dogs are happier because they're appreciated

The positive behavior of follower dogs gets noticed—by you and by other people. Dogs recognize smiles and appreciative tones of voice and thrive on the attention.

Follower dogs are happier because they can go more places

Well-behaved follower dogs are easier to bring along when you go visiting and are often allowed to remain in places where a dog causing a ruckus would be kicked out.

Follower dogs are happier because they know the consequences of every behavior

Follower dogs know which of their behaviors bring praise, petting, and rewards, and which behaviors bring scolding. This black-and-white understanding helps them choose which behaviors to do, and which ones to avoid.

Follower dogs are happier because they learn what your "human sounds" mean

Like anyone who learns a foreign language, dogs feel confident and empowered when they understand what you're saying.

Finally, follower dogs are SMARTER because their brain has been developed

Teaching your dog ANYTHING spurs his brain to build mental connections, which makes him more successful at learning additional things. In other words, his intelligence and learning skills start to snowball with the very first thing you teach and keep snowballing with each new word.

Now…what dog wouldn't love all that?

Kathy: "But why do I have to be my dog's leader to teach him things? Won't he learn from me if I just love him? Don't dogs want to please the people they love?"

Michele (smiling): "Dogs want to please the people they RESPECT. They want to please leaders. Dogs take advantage of non-leaders. Or ignore them. Or simply co-exist with them in a sort of limbo."

They will love you either way—because dogs don't equate love with respect.

> Dogs love blindly. They respect only those who have earned it. So teaching them to respect you will in no way diminish their love for you—and if you want to take proper care of them, teaching them to respect you is mandatory.

So if you already have your dog's respect

 You need to know what to do to keep it.

And if you've lost his respect

 You need to know what to do to get it back.

Kathy (smiling, too): "Okay, I think I understand **why** I need to teach Jake how to be a good follower. Now tell me **how!**"

How to teach your dog to be a follower

Teaching your dog to respect you—to be a good follower—means teaching him vocabulary words, along with the rules and routines of your household.

"TOY!"

As you're teaching him these words, rules, and routines—and more importantly, as you're requiring him to LEARN these words, rules, and routines—he will come to recognize and respect you as a capable teacher and leader.

When he respects you, he will automatically adjust his daily behaviors to better ones. Why? Simply because that's what dogs do.

Vocabulary + Rules = A Good Dog

Teaching your dog vocabulary words, rules, and routines means **educating** him.

Educated dogs are the happiest, smartest, most confident dogs in the world. They have learned so many words, routines, and good behaviors that they fully understand what is expected of them.

- Educated dogs know what to do.
- Educated dogs know what NOT to do.

Dogs love the security of knowing what to do and what not to do. And their **teacher** is the person they come to view as their trusted leader. They look up to that person. They believe in that person. They trust that person to do anything with them, to handle them in any way necessary.

You want yourself to be that person. Which is why YOU must always be the one to train your dog.

You've heard of dog training schools that promise to take your dog to their establishment and train him for you, then send him home to you?

I wouldn't even consider this. Dogs aren't robots who can be programmed by someone else to listen to you and do what you say. Dogs listen to you and do what you say when they **respect** you—and they respect you only when you are the teacher and leader who **earns** their respect.

No one else can do that for you. You have to do it yourself.

 An educated dog is a true companion, while an uneducated dog is just a casual pet.

If you don't educate your dog

He will never be the dog he could have been. He will always be less intelligent, less aware of his own worth and abilities.

 You know the old saying—a mind is a terrible thing to waste!

An educated dog is a thinking dog. He looks at you and reads your facial expressions and body language. He listens carefully. He pieces together individual words into complex actions.

"Where's your rope toy, Buffy? Where is it? Go find it. Oops, not quite, that's your hedgehog toy. Drop it. Go find your rope toy. Is it upstairs? Go upstairs! Upstairs! Get your rope toy. Good girl, you got it! Bring it here. Good! Now give it to me. Drop it! Good girl! Yay!"

Interested in a dog like that? Good for you! My dogs are like that—and yours can be, too.

First, your dog has to learn the meaning of all those words. That's where you—and this book—come in.

How to teach your dog words

Is it really possible for a dog to learn human words?

Yes, he will learn words easily—if you consistently **link** a word to its appropriate object or action.

Dogs learn language just as babies do, you see. You hold up a teddy bear to your baby and say *teddy* over and over.

Now imagine if you said *teddy* to your baby—but never held up the teddy bear. Your baby wouldn't have the slightest idea what it meant. Until you connect a word with an object or action, words are only **meaningless sounds**.

Think about that. It's very important.

When you listen to a conversation in a foreign language, you can't understand it. Because…

Libkajuko skapapule!

The words are not connected to anything concrete. The foreigner chatters on and on without pointing to anything in the real world. Don't foreign languages always sound impossibly fast? They sound like one long run-on sentence, with no way to tell the words apart.

That's what English sounds like to your dog.

But let's say you're speaking with a French gentleman and he repeats a single sound—one sound only—*pom*. He repeats it clearly and distinctly, while holding up an apple and showing it to you. You'd get it, wouldn't you? You wouldn't know how to spell it—it's actually spelled POMME—but you'd understand that the sound *pom* refers to the round red fruit with the stem and green leaves.

The sound has become a word.
A word is simply a sound with meaning.

So...to turn a sound into a word for your dog

1. Emphasize the sound clearly and distinctly.
2. Repeatedly show the object to your dog, or help him do the action or behavior.

Chapter 3

The Most Important Word to Teach

Word #1: "No"

When you tell your dog "No", you want him to learn:

- that this particular behavior is not allowed
- that he must stop the behavior
- that he must not repeat it

You might think that's pretty obvious, right? Isn't "No" such a simple word that your dog should understand it the first time you say it?

Not at all. Your dog was not born understanding English. To your dog, *no* isn't a word at all—it's just a **sound**, and like all other sounds, it's meaningless until you show him—repeatedly—that it has a **meaning**.

Suppose you're watching TV. When a commercial comes on, you wander into the kitchen for a glass of water. Through the window you see your dog Jake digging a hole in the tulip bed. You raise the window and shout, "Jake, no! No!"

Jake looks up, startled. He stops digging. You step away from the window and you wait, watching.

If Jake resumes digging, you slip out the side door and pick up the garden hose that you've coiled there for just this purpose. You tip-toe across the lawn just far enough to get into range. You shout, "No! No!" as you turn on the water and spray Jake's hind end. He leaps into the air and scrambles away as you repeat, "No. No digging!"

Here's what Jake learned

He was digging. Unfamiliar sounds floated through the air. He continued to dig—and suddenly, mysteriously, he got soaked from behind, and boy, was he startled!

Jake thinks about it. The harsh sound *no* occurred AS he was digging. Hmm. Perhaps his digging **produced** the sound, which was then followed by a startling blast of water. Clearly the sound should be considered a warning of some kind. Yes, indeed, he will definitely become more alert the next time he hears that sound. In fact, maybe he shouldn't dig at all, in case it was his digging that caused the sound—and the water—to occur....

Jake is well on his way to making the correct association that *no* is a sound with meaning—and that its meaning is a warning or admonition.

How to make "No" mean something

You might be thinking, "But I say 'No' all the time, yet my dog doesn't stop what he's doing!"

That's right, if all you do is SAY it, it will remain a meaningless sound. Remember, to become a **meaningful word**, you have to connect a sound to something tangible—preferably something memorable.

With Jake, we accomplished that by sneaking out with the hose. We could also have tried charging out with a squirt gun and Indian war whoops.

The point is to add something startling or unpleasant to the sound *no* so it takes on **meaning** and becomes a **word**.

> In other words, reinforce or "back up" your "No" with something that makes an impression on your dog. This reinforcement or "back-up" is called a **correction**.

Correction #1: Back up your "No" with Stern Body Language

This is the mildest of all corrections and it's the one to start with, with virtually every dog and every unacceptable behavior. In fact, for some dogs and many unacceptable behaviors, Stern Body Language will be the only correction you'll ever need.

Here's what I mean by Stern Body Language:

- Draw yourself up to your full height.
- Put your hands on your hips.
- Lean forward toward your dog.
- Pull your eyebrows together into a fierce frown.
- Stare into your dog's eyes and clip out your "No!" in a deep baritone voice.

For example, if your dog gets into the trash, turn on your Stern Body Language, lead him firmly to the overturned trash barrel (act melodramatic—dogs and small children respond well to it), and say sternly, "No!"

Honestly, many dogs—especially young puppies and gentle, sensitive adult dogs—never need anything more than this. So give your dog the benefit of the doubt and start out with this one. If he responds to it, excellent!

Correction #2: Back up your "No" with a Collar Shake and/or Time Out

If you find your dog back in the trash ten minutes later, repeat the Stern Body Language but add a quick (one-second) shake of his collar. (Caution: Don't do this with an aggressive dog! Instead, hire a local trainer.) After the quick collar shake, put your dog in his crate for a 15-minute Time Out while you clean up the mess.

> ☀ Time Outs can be as useful for dogs as they are for
> children. Time Outs also give YOU a chance to calm
> down after your dog has done something bad.

Some trainers will tell you, "Never use your dog's crate as punishment, because then he will dislike the crate and won't want to sleep in it."

Nonsense. I've always used the crate for Time Outs and my dogs still love the privacy of their "den," into which they go voluntarily to relax and sleep.

Correction #3: Back up your "No" with a squirt of water

You've already seen this one in action. For many dogs, a sudden spray of water from a plastic spray bottle or squirt gun is one of the most effective reinforcers of the word "No." It's especially persuasive for small dogs. Also, by the way, for many cats!

Unfortunately, some dogs pay no mind to the pathetic little squirts of a typical squirt gun. You can buy heavy-duty water cannons that look like submachine guns, but obviously not for indoor use unless you don't mind living in Waterworld.

However, these big water guns work well outdoors. For example:

- for a dog who's digging holes in the garden
- for a dog who's getting into the trash barrel
- for a dog who's standing on the back porch barking

A garden hose also works, though it can be awkward to get to quickly and silently. Often your dog has stopped his unacceptable behavior by the time you've gotten the hose uncoiled and turned on.

For chronic offenders, clever owners hang a hose directly outside the back door, with the water always turned on and a hose control that allows for instant on-off when you flick the switch.

I do have to rain on your parade here by telling you that some dogs enjoy being squirted. So this correction doesn't always hold water. So to speak.

Correction #4: Back up your "No" with a sudden loud sound

If you follow up your "No" with a vigorous hand clap, or shaking a can full of pennies, some dogs will stop a bad behavior.

The Barker Breaker® by Amtek is a commercial "beeper" that you hold in your hand and activate by pressing the button. It produces a loud high-pitched sound that makes many dogs scramble away from whatever behavior they were engaging in. I've found it to be very effective. (Just be forewarned that it's loud and shrill for human ears, too!) Visit *www.amtekpet.com* for more information.

A plastic fly swatter is another effective sound-maker when *thwacked!* against a table or wall.

Correction #5: Back up your "No" with balled-up socks tossed at your dog's hind end

It's the harmless but unexpected pop on the rear end that makes many dogs think twice about repeating the behavior that caused it.

If you want your dog to know where the correction came from, stare firmly at him when he whips around in surprise. Repeat "No" for good measure.

 "Are there times when you don't want your dog to know where a correction came from?"

Yes, some dogs are more impressed when a correction seems to come out of nowhere. If you say absolutely nothing and simply pop your dog's hind end from across the room, then immediately go back to reading your paper, humming nonchalantly, not even looking at him, your dog may conclude that the correction is a natural consequence of that particular behavior.

> In other words, the behavior itself is correcting him! If he believes this, he is more likely to avoid the behavior even when you're not in the room.

So which physical correction should you use?

We've looked at five **corrections** (reinforcers) for the word "No." Which one should you use?

As I said earlier, start with the gentlest one—stern body language. If that doesn't work, pick one of the others.

 A proper correction should make your dog stop the behavior, drop his tail, flatten his ears, and shrink his body a bit in submission. His facial expression and body language should say, "Oops! Sorry about that!"

If he flings himself onto his back, dribbling urine, you came on much too strong. Don't do that again!

If he keeps right on doing what he's doing, or if he stops for a moment, then goes back to the misbehavior as soon as you turn your back, you need to choose a stronger correction. Or combine two of them.

> Let your DOG be the one to tell you—through his expression and body language, but most of all, through the RESULTS—which correction is most suitable for him. Every dog is different.

Caution: If you try these corrections for a couple of weeks and your dog is still unresponsive, you should consult with a professional trainer. He or she can evaluate your dog personally and help you figure out what's going on.

Eight common mistakes when teaching "No"

1. Repeatedly saying "No" without backing it up.
2. Trying to teach your dog that "No" means "ethically or morally wrong."
3. Repeating the same correction even when it obviously doesn't make your dog stop the behavior.
4. Asking your dog to stop what he's doing—instead of telling him.
5. Smiling or laughing when you say "No."
6. Petting your dog while correcting him.
7. Calling your dog to come to you when you're planning to correct him.
8. Chasing your dog so you can catch him and correct him.

Let's look at these mistakes one at a time.

Don't say "No" without being willing and able to back it up

When her TV show went to commercial, Kathy wandered into the kitchen for a glass of water. Through the window she saw her dog Jake digging another hole in the tulip bed. She raised the window. "Jake, no! No!" Jake stopped digging and looked up but Kathy was already hurrying back to the TV with her water. Jake resumed his digging.

Here's what Jake learned from Kathy's "correction":

That when he does certain things that are enjoyable to him, his owner's head sometimes appears, and vague sounds float out of her mouth.

Nothing else happens.

Jake logically concludes that the sound *no* is a coincidental background sound—like the incidental sounds of flying dirt he hears when he digs a hole. The sound *no* carries no consequences, so he can ignore it, just like he ignores the sound of the flying dirt. Just another one of life's little mysteries!

> If you say "No" and don't back it up by doing whatever it takes to make your dog stop the behavior, you're teaching him that "No" is a meaningless sound that can be ignored.

Be especially careful when you're occupied with doing something like watching TV or talking on the phone. Some dogs learn that if you're busy, you may yell at them, but you won't make them stop. Not a good lesson!

Don't try to teach your dog that "No" means "wrong"

You may be wondering: "How can I get my dog to understand which things are the **right** things to do, and which things are the **wrong** things to do?"

The answer is: You can't. Your dog will never understand that some things are morally and ethically right, while other things are morally and ethically wrong.

To your dog, there will never be anything inherently "wrong" with grabbing a toy from another pet. You can't teach him values, such as Sharing Is Kind. You can't teach him to step into another living creature's shoes and empathize with their feelings.

Kathy held up her ruined sandal and waved it at her dog Jake.

"Jake, now you look at this! These sandals cost me seventy-five dollars and now you've ruined them! They were a perfect match for my turquoise outfit! It was wrong of you to do this, Jake! It was mean! You've made me very unhappy and you darned well better be sorry! Are you listening to me, Jake? Do you understand me?"

Poor Jake. All he understands is that his owner is holding up a chew toy and spewing out a long monologue of harmless sounds. As she waves the sandal around, he stares longingly at it. He remembers where he got this tasty toy. He also remembers that there were lots more in the same place.

Don't bother asking your dog silly questions:

- "Don't you know that your sister Fluffy will feel sad if you steal her toy?"
- "Can't you see that jumping on my white pants upsets me?"
- "Don't you understand that chewing up my Beanie Babies is a mean thing to do?"

This is how your dog would answer those questions:

- "Huh?"
- "Huh?"
- "Huh?"

Don't think of your dog's behaviors as right or wrong. Think of them as **acceptable** to you—or **unacceptable** to you. When you correct an unacceptable behavior, don't try to explain WHY it's unacceptable. Just use the sound *no* and turn it into a meaningful word by backing it up with a correction.

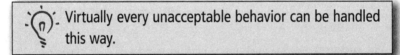

> Virtually every unacceptable behavior can be handled this way.

Don't keep using a correction if it doesn't work for your dog

It's tempting to choose a particular correction—for example, the squirt gun—because you like it. But the question should always be: Does it work for your dog?

Jake story

The Armstrongs were sick of Jake's incessant chewing. Their living room upholstery was beginning to look like Craters-of-the-Moon. So Roger bought a plastic squirt gun, and when he caught Jake chewing, he ran toward the dog, squirting madly.

Well! That was just fine and dandy with Jake! He leaped happily into the air, trying to catch the water with his tongue. The "game" ended when Roger, backpedaling frantically, tripped over the ottoman and fell on his backside. An hour later, Roger returned to the living room and found a fresh hole dug in the sofa. Jake was curled up in it, chewing on the plastic squirt gun.

This happens a lot. Owners will complain that they tried the squirt gun (or fly swatter or collar shake) again and again. And it didn't work.

- Now, sometimes there is something amiss with their **timing**. They may not have been quick enough in applying the correction in close enough proximity to the unacceptable behavior. Timing is critical.

- Or there might be something amiss with their **body language**—their attitude as they're carrying out the correction. They may not be acting stern enough or serious enough. Dogs can tell when your heart really isn't in a correction.
- And sometimes **consistency** is the problem. If you correct your dog for a behavior one day, but allow him to do it the next day without any correction, he will never understand.

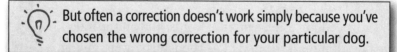 But often a correction doesn't work simply because you've chosen the wrong correction for your particular dog.

**Your dog will show you,
by his body language and by the results,
if a particular correction works for him.**

Dogs will do what is most to their advantage to do. If your dog believes that the **fun** of doing a particular misbehavior outweighs the **discomfort** he receives from a particular correction, he will keep doing the misbehavior.

Only when the discomfort of the correction outweighs the fun of the misbehavior will he stop doing the misbehavior—because he believes it is no longer worth it—to HIM.

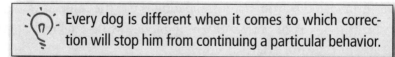 Every dog is different when it comes to which correction will stop him from continuing a particular behavior.

You should strive for the gentlest correction that will stop the misbehavior, but ultimately...

it is your DOG who is the decider of which correction that must be.

Don't ASK your dog to stop what he's doing

As Kathy struggled to pull another sandal out of Jake's mouth, she tried to reason with him. "Ja-a-a-a-k-e," she pleaded. "Come on now, Jake, be a good boy? Let me have this, Jake. Be a good boy?"

Her wheedling tone, clutter of words, and all the indecisive question marks sounded as though she were giving Jake a choice. His answer was to wag his tail, clamp down, and tug more firmly.

> Your tone of voice means everything to your dog. Keep your "No" short and uncluttered, your voice deep and serious. This is more difficult for women, which is why dogs often respond better to a man's corrective voice than to a woman's.

But don't shout. Dogs interpret shouting as loss of control and they conclude that you are a screechy, blustering person not worthy of respect.

Or they become so fearful that their survival instinct kicks in and they freeze up and become unable to think. A dog in the throes of fear is intimidated by you, but intimidation is not the same as respect. A respectful dog is in perfect learning mode, while a fearful dog is incapable of learning a darned thing.

Don't smile or laugh when you say "No"

Roger couldn't help chuckling as he pulled Jake
away from the spitting cat.

"Hey, Jake," Roger said. "Leave the cat alone." But
he had to admit that it had been thrilling to watch
his athletic dog in full pursuit. Roger wasn't fond of cats,
anyway.

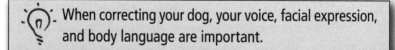

Jake looked up at him, panting and grinning. He could
tell by Roger's smile and relaxed body language that he wasn't really in
trouble—that in fact, his master approved of his behavior.

If you secretly think it's cute or funny when your dog does something
you don't want him to repeat, you need to keep those thoughts off your
face and out of your voice. Otherwise, your dog will "read" your true
belief and conclude that your "No" isn't really serious.

Again I remind you to match your stern voice with stern body
language:

- Draw yourself up to your full height.
- Put your hands on your hips.
- Lean forward toward your dog.
- Pull your eyebrows together into a fierce frown.
- Stare into your dog's eyes and clip out your "No!" in a deep
  baritone voice.

> When correcting your dog, your voice, facial expression,
> and body language are important.

Don't add affection or petting to your corrections

"Jake, how many times have I told you to stay off the sofa!" Kathy complained. She wrapped her arm around the dog and pushed him onto the floor, her hand sliding along his back in a stroking motion. When he was down, she tickled his head. As she headed for the kitchen, Jake jumped back onto the sofa.

Many dogs are happy to "take a correction" if it includes personal attention and touching. In fact, if they think you might pick them up or pet them during or immediately after correcting them, some dogs will deliberately misbehave just to get the petting afterward!

So make your corrections swift and impersonal.

- Don't smile at your dog.
- Don't pick him up.
- Don't rest your hand on him while you're scolding him.

Simply correct him, then turn your attention away from him and go about your business. You want him to learn that only when he is behaving well does he get personal attention, smiling, touching, holding, and petting.

Don't call your dog if you're going to correct him

This is one of the most common mistakes made by dog owners!

If you call your dog and he comes to you, and then you scold him or do anything unpleasant with him, he will associate the sound *come* with discomfort and he will thereafter be reluctant to respond positively to that sound.

> You never want your dog to think that obeying "Come" might cause discomfort.

And don't try to trick your dog by adopting a wheedling, coaxing tone: "Come here, Jake, Mommy's not going to hurt you, come on, sweetheart."

Because if your dog follows his trusting nature and believes you—and then discovers your deception—he will not only distrust the word "Come" but also he will distrust YOU.

No, whenever you need to correct your dog or do anything uncomfortable with him, don't call him.

Go get him. Silently.

And if your dog runs away from you when you're going to get him?

Don't chase your dog

When the garbage can crashed to the kitchen floor, strewing trash everywhere, Jake knew he was in trouble. Kathy was rushing toward him, hands outstretched. Jake feinted left, and rushed right. The chase was on!

When they don't want to be caught, many dogs will dart just out of your reach and lead you on merry chases around the house.

You should never play this game!

Promise yourself right now that you will never again run after your dog—because every second that he eludes you cheapens you in his eyes. He knows that he is defeating your efforts and making you look like a bumbling fool.

Instead, **track him down silently**. Don't run. Walk firmly and purposefully, leaning forward with intent, keeping your expression stony-faced, drilling your dog with your eyes.

Most dogs are baffled and unnerved by such persistent, methodical following. In fact, many dogs eventually shrink down and give up, and if your dog does this, make your correction much milder to encourage this kind of yielding behavior.

Some dogs will actually freeze in position whenever they're caught doing something unacceptable. They've learned through experience that you will track them down, to the ends of the earth if necessary, to give a deserved correction, so they figure they might as well stop and get it over with!

Now, let's assume your dog has given up and/or you have him absolutely cornered so you can be sure of getting hold of his collar without any risk of lunging at him and missing. What should you do next?

1. Lead him briskly to the scene of the crime (the stolen food, the chewed slippers, the housebreaking mess).

    As you lead him, give his collar a few corrective jerks so he can tell you're not happy with him. But use common sense! You would jerk a Chihuahua's collar with one finger—just a tiny little tug—and you would jerk a submissive dog or first offender much more gently than a feisty, dominant, or repeat offender.

2. Show your dog the bad deed and tell him firmly, "No." Another shake of his collar for emphasis, then either put him in his crate for a 15-minute Time Out (if you need to clean up some mess) or just let his collar go and don't spare him a second glance. If he tries to make up by fawning around your feet with a sorrowful look, ignore him.

 Your coldness at this time will impress upon him how serious you are about unacceptable behaviors.

"My dog dances out of reach almost every time I reach toward him—what should I do?"

A hand-hold will help solve this problem.

A hand-hold is a piece of light rope or sturdy string attached to your dog's buckle collar. It should be just long enough to swing short of the ground when he walks. (You don't want him stepping on it and jerking his own neck.) Some people cut an old cotton leash to the proper length and clip it to the collar.

A dog who consistently runs from you should wear a hand-hold whenever you're around to supervise him. Be sure to take off the hand-hold when you have to leave him unsupervised—you don't want it getting hung up on something when you're not around to notice and help.

Chase games in general

You yourself (or your spouse or kids or whoever owned your dog before you) may have taught your dog to run away from you—by playing chase games with him. If you make little teasing lunges toward your dog, or playfully stamp your foot at him, and he dashes away from you, both of you undoubtedly think this is a lot of fun.

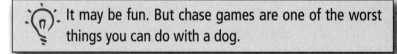

It may be fun. But chase games are one of the worst things you can do with a dog.

Lunging at your dog and pretending you're going to grab him teaches him that when you move toward him, he can evade you—exactly what you don't want him to learn!

"What if my dog chases ME or my kids? Sometimes we run and he runs after us."

It depends on how your dog is doing the chasing:

If he's an otherwise well-behaved dog, and if, when you stop running, he settles down quickly, that's fine. When HE chases YOU, you're being the leader and he's being the follower. All well and good.

But if chase games get him so excited or intense that he nips at your legs or slams his body against yours or tangles up your feet, that's bad.

Or if you stop playing and he won't settle down but keeps running in circles around you or keeps trying to goad you into playing some more, that's bad.

Now, some dogs just need to hear "No" a few times (reinforced by a physical correction if necessary) and they'll cease their nipping or over-excitable behaviors.

But other dogs (often herding breeds, sighthounds, or terriers) can't handle any kind of chase game. Their instincts to get rough or grab are just too strong.

> **Warning:** Children should not play any kind of chase game with a dog. Period. Children can't judge when a dog is out of control and they can't correct a dog with enough authority when his behavior goes over the line.

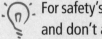 For safety's sake, don't allow your dog to chase any child, and don't allow your kids to run away from your dog.

Ah-ah! (and other words that mean "No")

Well, we've certainly spent a lot of time on "No", haven't we?

That's because it's the one word you need to **control** your dog. You must be able to stop your dog from doing anything you don't want him to do.

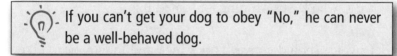

> If you can't get your dog to obey "No," he can never be a well-behaved dog.

But "No" isn't the only word you might use to stop your dog from doing some unacceptable behavior. There are other words and phrases you can use as substitutes—and some of these are even better than "No."

Word #2: "Ah-ah!"

Anyone who has raised a child is intimately familiar with this guttural sound. It's a natural expression of warning and rebuke and it's perfect for misbehaviors that happen suddenly and unexpectedly.

For example, you're cleaning tartar off your dog's teeth with a dental pick. He starts to pull his head away. You need to stop this movement ASAP so you don't accidentally chip his gum. "Ah-ah!" bursts from your throat more quickly than you can form your lips around "No." Try it right now, for practice. Make it a quick, choppy, urgent sound.

For many owners, "Ah-ah!" is actually a better word to use than "No." If you've been saying "No" to your dog for a long time (without knowing how to enforce it), it may have become a long-standing habit for him to ignore it. Starting fresh with "Ah-ah!", where now you know how to back it up with something physical, is a great idea.

Word #3: "Stop That"

I often use this phrase with a dog who is being persistent and annoying, such as...

- a dog who keeps insisting on being petted
- a dog who keeps wriggling when I'm grooming him
- a dog who keeps whining for something

Your voice should convey annoyance and indignation. Likewise your facial expression. Don't smile or chuckle.

 Correcting a dog effectively means being an actor! Your tone of voice and facial expression are important.

Word #4: "Don't Touch"

Suppose you've caught your dog chewing on your sneaker. Take it away and say "No!" as you hold it melodramatically near his face. Now add a slow, ominous "Don't...touch." It's a phrase that comes naturally, so you'll probably say it with feeling.

You can also use "Don't touch" as a pre-emptive warning to let your dog know that something is off limits. For example, you bring home a caged hamster and show it to your dog, warning him "Don't...touch" and reinforcing physically, if necessary, until he backs away and looks like he "gets" it. With "Don't touch," you want to convey the message that the object in question is very important to you and is to be treated like one of your personal belongings:

- precious to YOU
- forbidden to HIM

Word #5: "Leave It"

When you go for a walk, does your dog snuffle along the ground for things to pick up and eat?

Sooner or later, a Vacuum Cleaner Dog will snatch up a piece of chocolate, which is toxic to dogs. Or a cigarette butt. Chewing gum. Aluminum foil. A piece of glass.

Nip this bad habit in the bud with "Leave it."

> ☀ "Leave it" is most useful when your dog is on a leash so you can reinforce with a sharp tug that turns him away from the temptation.

If he has a weakness for some particular delicacy, you can even stage a "set-up." Drop the temptation on the sidewalk and practice walking your dog past it, correcting him whenever he tries to nose it, or lick it, or pick it up.

"Leave it" is also a great phrase to use

- When your dog is sniffing another dog and you suddenly see somebody's hackles coming up. You want your dog away from there right now!
- When your dog is pestering the cat or rooting around in the laundry basket.

- When you're walking your male dog inside a pet supply store and he's sniffing with interest at a display stand where, no doubt, other male dogs have left their "calling card."

You can easily come up with other situations where you'd like your dog to immediately stop what he's doing and move on to something else. That's the time for "Leave it."

Word #6: "Hey!"

I doubt you'll find this word in any other training book. Nevertheless, it's one of the most common words used by dog owners and trainers alike. Really.

"Hey!" is a warning word that essentially means, "Hey!"

Seriously, that's what it means. I use it to get my dog's attention when I can't quite tell what she's doing but I have a concern that it might be something I don't want her to do. I want to get her attention quickly so I can intervene if necessary.

For example:

- She's sniffing at the floor around the trash can. Could I have thrown something away and missed the can? "Hey!"
- One of my dogs has finished her supper. The other dog has not. The greedy eater is sidling surreptitiously toward the slowpoke, hoping to sneak her head into the bowl and snitch a few bites. "Hey!"

Many of these corrective words can be used interchangeably. That's fine. You'll sort out on your own which words and phrases work better for you and your dog and a particular misbehavior.

Whichever corrective word you choose, remember, **TONE OF VOICE** is all-important!

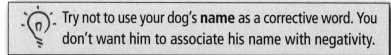 Try not to use your dog's **name** as a corrective word. You don't want him to associate his name with negativity.

Now we come to a corrective word that some trainers consider taboo (though most of them probably use it anyway, when no one can hear them!):

Word #7: "Bad"

This is a controversial word because it's used like so: "Bad dog! Shame on you!" Child psychologists tell us we're not supposed to call our **kids** bad, that children internalize our words and form negative self-images based on our negative characterizations of them as people.

This doesn't really hold for dogs, who are far too rooted in the moment to do this kind of deep self-analysis. No matter how bluntly you tell a dog that he is the very son of Satan, he won't start moping about his self-image and thinking of himself as worthless.

On the other hand, using the phrase "Bad dog" might put YOU in such a negative mood that you start thinking of your misbehaving dog as **inherently** bad. As though he was born a bad dog and will always be a bad dog.

This is not a constructive attitude at all.

So if your relationship with your dog isn't very good right now, you should probably avoid using the word "bad" to describe any of his behaviors. It will only make it that much harder for you to see your dog in a positive light.

But if your relationship is fine and you believe that he is inherently a good dog, then you're not going to do any harm by occasionally reacting to some particularly odious behavior with the outraged phrase, "What did you do? BAD dog. Shame on you!"

"Bad dog!" is an honest human expression and we all use it from time to time—yes, even the trainers who tell you not to!

Chapter 4

Happy Words of Praise

Word #8: "Good!"

"Good dog!" "Good puppy!" "Good boy!" "Good girl!"

Doesn't that sound nice? It's about time we got around to praising our dog, isn't it?

> You don't want to be in Correction Mode all day long, just waiting for your dog to make some little mistake so you can pounce on him! What a miserable existence that would be, for both of you. No, if you're going to let your dog know which behaviors are **unacceptable,** you must also let him know which behaviors are **acceptable**—even desirable.

Watch for **good behavior**! Praise your dog whenever he does something you like—even if it's just resting quietly on his blanket, or chewing on his bone, or sitting peacefully beside the cat.

"GOOD boy, Jake! GOOD dog! GOOD bone!"

Notice how you can use **GOOD** to refer not only to your DOG, but also to the good thing he's doing.

"GOOD sit!" "GOOD come!"

Five tips for praising your dog

1. **Pitch your voice higher than usual.** A low-pitched, serious "Good dog" sounds more like a growl than praise. Dogs love cheerful tones, which is why they often respond better to a woman's praise than a man's. Brighten your voice when you're telling your dog what a GOOD dog he is.

2. **Exaggerate each syllable.** Draw out your praise words. "Gooood giiiiirl." Brisk, clipped words sound more like commands or reprimands. S-t-r-e-t-c-h out your praise words so your dog can savor them.

3. **Add a physical "back-up" to your praise words.** Just as you add a physical reinforcement to your correction words, add a physical component to your praise words—a pat on the head, a tickle under the chin, a rub of the chest, a moment of silly play, or a treat.

4. **Smile when you praise your dog.** Many dogs are astute observers and can see, hear, and recognize a smile.

5. **Tell your dog he's a good "puppy."** Yes, even after he's all grown up! The word *puppy* makes you think of cuteness, fuzziness, and playful antics, and your voice will take on a fond tone that older dogs enjoy. Trust me, it will make both of you feel happy.

One of my favorite praise words is:

Word #9: "Yay!"

"Yay!" is a terrific word to use whenever your dog starts to do something right and you want to reassure him that he's on the right track.

For example, when he's learning how to climb stairs and he puts his paw tentatively onto a new tread, encourage him with a cheerful, "YAY! That's it! GOOD boy!"

Also use "Yay!" when your dog is successful at something you've been working on. For example, after a successful housebreaking trip, "Yay! You did it!" will let your dog know that he has accomplished something that really pleased you.

YAY! Your dog has learned nine words and phrases so far, all related to correction and praise. These nine words are an essential foundation for raising a good dog. They show him with absolute clarity the consequences of everything he does—positive and negative.

Dogs learn almost entirely by

- the consequences of their actions
- your reactions to their actions

If you always attach **positive** reactions and **positive** consequences to his **positive** behaviors…

and if you always attach **negative** reactions and **negative** consequences to his **negative** behaviors…

your dog will choose to do the positive behaviors and avoid the negative behaviors. Because it is to his advantage to do so—and that's what dogs do.

> So even if your dog learned only these nine words and no others, he would be very much under control and quite a well-behaved dog.

But we have 91 more words to teach him!

Chapter 5

Learn About Your Breed

Before we continue teaching your dog words, you should find out something about the typical temperament and behavior of your dog's breed.

Why your dog's breed matters

Your dog does certain things because they are "hardwired" into his genes.

Let me explain.

Most breeds were developed for a reason, and that reason usually had to do with working ability, such as herding sheep, killing rodents in the barn, chas-
ing rabbits, treeing raccoons, flushing pheasant, retrieving shot ducks, pulling carts and sleds, guarding and protecting, and so on.

When developing breeds for working purposes, breeders found that certain behavioral traits best suited each type of work. By only breeding together dogs who had these behavioral characteristics, these behaviors became "hardwired" into your breed's genes.

Working behaviors include:

- high energy level for working all day
- chasing and grabbing things that move (running children and other animals, bikes, cars)
- aggression toward other animals
- digging holes
- barking, baying, howling
- suspiciousness toward strangers
- instincts to explore, escape, and follow their eyes and nose in search of adventure
- ignoring your commands in favor of making their own decisions

Good news and bad news about working behaviors

The good news about working behaviors is this: If you want a dog for, say, hunting or herding, you can choose a purebred who was developed to do that type of work and there's a decent chance he will have inherited those behavioral genes.

The bad news about working behaviors is this: If you just want a family companion, working behaviors can be a real nuisance, and because they're hardwired into the genes, they can be very difficult to change.

  "But isn't a dog's **environment**—the way he's raised—more important than heredity?"

With some dogs, yes. When well-raised and well-trained, many dogs with a genetic predisposition for undesirable characteristics may not express those characteristics.

But with other dogs, NO—their genetic tendencies are too strong to be changed. "Managed" to some extent, perhaps. But not changed.

For example, many Akitas and Pit Bull Terriers (certainly not all, but many) will never tolerate another dog of the same sex, or a cat, no matter how hard you try. In fact, trying at all may lead to serious injury or death of the other pet.

Temperament and behavior are definitely **influenced** by environment, which includes how you raise and train your dog. But also important—and in some dogs, MORE important—is innate genetic temperament. Everything starts with the genes your dog was born with.

And take heed! The influence of environment can work AGAINST you, too. If you choose a breed whose genes include characteristics you want, but then you screw up his raising and training (especially during the most important formative period of seven to sixteen weeks old), those desirable characteristics you thought you were getting when you chose this breed can go straight out the window!

To sum up: Both genetics and environment are influential in how your dog turns out. But within any individual dog, one of these influences is often stronger than the other.

Breeds don't always act the way you might expect

And now…

After all this discussion about "typical" temperament and behavior, I need to kick sand all over your clean floor by telling you that some purebred dogs actually don't have the temperament and behaviors that are typical for their breed.

In other words, some purebreds don't conform to the norm.

In every breed, there are energetic individuals and placid individuals. Stubborn individuals and eager-to-please individuals. Dominant individuals and submissive individuals. Standoffish introverts and good-natured goofballs who love everybody.

 Purebred puppies, you see, are not guaranteed to grow up to have a certain temperament or set of behaviors.

Why not?

Some don't grow up with their breed's typical temperament because of how they were raised, especially during the most formative psychological period of seven to sixteen weeks old.

We just talked about this—that many aspects of temperament and behavior can be influenced by environment, more so in some dogs than in others.

Other dogs don't grow up with their breed's typical temperament because one or both of their **parents** didn't have the typical temperament genes for their breed. So they couldn't pass those genes on to their offspring.

Ironically, it's okay for a dog not to inherit the typical genes for his breed if they would have been for undesirable behavioral traits.

Take, for example, a Jack Russell Terrier's tendency to inherit genes for high energy and stubbornness. If your particular Jack Russell puppy happens to inherit genes for calmness and obedience, he would be a non-typical Jack Russell, but you'd probably appreciate it!

But non-typical genes can be bad if the behavior you were expecting was positive. For example, if you chose a Golden Retriever because you wanted a friendly, sociable dog, it would be very disappointing if your Golden puppy turned out to have inherited shy or aggressive genes.

> You can minimize this risk by not acquiring a purebred puppy unless you've personally evaluated both parents to ensure that they have the traits you're looking for in your puppy.

If you want to be even more certain of temperament, acquire an adult dog rather than a puppy. There are plenty of adult dogs who have already proven themselves to have the characteristics you want. If you find such an adult, often from a breed rescue group or animal shelter, don't let "typical breed negatives" worry you. When you acquire an adult, you're acquiring what he already IS.

So now you know that not all purebred dogs have the temperament and behavior you might expect for their breed. But don't get sidetracked by this **possibility**. Unless you know for sure that it's true for your particular dog—that your Akita is very different from other Akitas, for example—you should assume that he is similar to other Akitas and you should find out what the breed was developed to do, so you will be better able to predict the behavioral traits your dog is likely to have.

By knowing what to expect from your breed, you will be aware of potential trouble areas. For example, when your terrier starts digging holes, you'll know that it will be harder to get him to obey "No" than it would be with a digging Pug. Terriers were bred to dig. Pugs were not.

Visit my website (*www.yourpurebredpuppy.com*) for honest reviews of 180 breeds.

If you discover that your breed is stubborn or independent, don't despair! By teaching your dog new words and backing up what you say, you will show him that you are a capable teacher/leader who is worth respecting. Even a stubborn, independent dog will understand this.

**A dog is always inclined
to please someone he respects.**

So even if your breed is challenging to work with in the beginning, don't give up. The first words are always the hardest for stubborn dogs and slow learners. By the time you get to the words further along in this book, your dog will have gotten the hang of the concept that sounds have meaning—and YOU will have gotten the hang of how to get across to him the meaning of each new sound.

Teaching and learning will become faster and easier for both of you!

Chapter 6

Schedule of Training

Which words to teach and when to teach them

At two to three months old, I teach a puppy

His daily routine. Where his food and water dishes are located. What times of day he will eat (typically morning, early afternoon, and evening). Where his bed is. What time he goes to bed. What time he gets up. Where he goes to the bathroom. Where his toys are kept. What routes he will be taken on for walks. And so on.

Dogs absolutely love routines. They feel safe and secure when they know where everything of importance is located in their world. They feel safe and secure when their lives follow a predictable schedule, and when they can count on you to say and do the same things again and again.

Routines reassure your dog that he knows what comes next, that his world is the same as it was yesterday, and that it will be the same tomorrow. Routines that **you** set tell your dog that **you** are the establisher of the rules and that he is the follower of the rules.

Start establishing routines in your dog's life right from the very beginning.

Correction words. To stop what he's doing when I say "No" or "Ah-ah" or "Stop that."

Praise words. What "Good!" and "Yay!" mean. (Puppies especially love the sound of "Yay!")

Crate training. To stay quietly in his crate at night when he goes to sleep, and during the day whenever I'm not interacting with him. (Not for more than two hours at a time during the day!)

Housebreaking. I immediately introduce a young puppy to his bathroom spot. However, he is still an infant and it will be some time before his internal organs are developed enough for reliability, especially during the day when his metabolism is high and he is running around and needing to "go" every few hours.

Toy breeds and hound breeds are especially slow to housebreak, with many not being reliable until eight to ten months of age.

Acceptance of being handled. I introduce the grooming positions of "Sit", "Stand", "Open your mouth", and "Give a paw" while I handle the puppy all over his body, brush his coat, brush his teeth, and clip his nails.

Food words. "Are you hungry?" "Supper!" "Biscuit!"

Gentleness. "Easy!" No biting. Take things gently from my hand. No grabbing.

At three to six months old, I teach a puppy

To lie down.

To STAY lying down for up to 30 minutes.

To look directly at me when I say his name.

To come when called.

To wait inside the door, even when it's open, until I tell him he can go through.

To walk on the leash without pulling.

To stop barking when I say "Quiet."

To interact politely with strangers and other animals.

To "Give" or "Drop" whatever is in his mouth when told.

Starting at six months old and up, I teach

The remaining words in this book, including advanced exercises, retrieving games, and tricks.

We're going to work our way through the vocabulary words pretty much in the order I just laid out. So if you have a young puppy, this is a good schedule to follow. If you have an adolescent or adult dog, you can use the same schedule in roughly the same order. Just skip over whatever words or behaviors your dog already knows.

Chapter 7

Respect Training

Establish consistent household rules

Establish one set of rules for your dog—what he can and cannot do. Everyone in your family should follow those same rules.

Here are some examples:

If YOU don't allow your dog upstairs, your spouse and kids can't allow it either.

If he can't sleep on the sofa on Monday, he can't sleep on it on Tuesday either.

If he can't jump on Aunt Martha when she comes visiting, then he can't jump on Uncle Fred either.

During these formative months of training, there should be no "maybes" or "sometimes." You may think you're being flexible by going back and forth about what your dog is allowed to do. Your dog, on the other hand, pegs you as **indecisive** and he will begin to test your rules to find out which ones are really rules, and which ones are up for grabs.

> 💡 **Dogs do not do well with gray areas.** If you allow one gray area, your dog is driven by instinct to second-guess another of your decisions, and another, and another, to find out where the limits really are.

Decide on the rules. Stick to them. Consistently. Everyone.

Use the same words

Everyone in your family should use the same words, and those words should mean the same thing to everyone.

In other words, don't do this

Roger says, "Jake, sit!"
Kathy says, "Sit down, Jake!"

Roger says, "Come, Jake!"
Kathy says, "Here, Jake!"

Roger asks, "Do you need to go out?"
Kathy asks, "Do you need to go potty?"

This is very confusing to your dog!

Don't do this, either

When Jake reared up and plunked his paws on Kathy's stomach, she said, "Down, Jake!" When she found him sleeping on forbidden furniture, she said, "Get down, Jake!" When he bounded up the stairs into the attic, she pointed at the stairs and said, "Jake, go down!"

Poor Jake. His owner is using the same word for three different actions. To make matters worse, none of those actions is what "Down" is supposed to mean.

When we get around to teaching "Down" to your dog, it will mean a lying down position. It will be much harder to teach this meaning if you're using that word to mean other things.

> As we work through our 100 words, go over each word with everyone in your family. Make sure you're all using the same word or phrase for the same behavior or object.

Don't talk too much

By now you've probably noticed how important it is to emphasize:

- SINGLE words.
- SHORT phrases.

In other words (How shall I put this kindly?), don't talk too much! This advice may be hard for chatty people to follow. But if you babble incessantly at your dog, he will struggle to pick out the few words he knows—the few words that really apply to him—from everything else you're saying. Trying to wade through all that "noise" is stressful and eventually he will start tuning you out because he believes that understanding you is hopeless. Obviously, this is not what you want!

So, during your dog's formative learning time, instead of rambling on and on about how your day went, use short sentences that emphasize one pertinent word or phrase.

"Are you **hungry**? Want your **supper**? Time for **supper**!"

"Do you need to go **out**? **Out** in the yard? Go **out**!"

"Want a **biscuit**? Here's your **biscuit**. Good **biscuit**!"

> When your dog trusts that you will use simple words that he understands, he will pay closer attention to you.

Later, when he's more settled and mature and further along in his training, go right ahead and pour out your heart to him when you need to—it's one of the reasons we love our dogs so much! But for now, keep your communication simple, i.e. short and sweet.

Don't allow sassiness

"Jake, sit!" "Bark!"

"Jake, sit down!" "Bark bark!"

Kathy tried to grab hold of his collar, but he danced just out of reach. He bowed his front end to the ground, hindquarters high in the air, tail wagging impishly. "Bark! Bark!" he shouted. Kathy sighed and went back to making toast for breakfast.

A dog who barks back at you when you tell him to do something is **sassing** you. This is as harmful to your relationship as it would be if your child exclaimed, "I don't want to! Make me!" and you ignored it.

If you have a sassing dog, put him on leash before you tell him to do anything. Or attach a hand-hold that he can wear all the time (under supervision). Leashes and hand-holds give you something to latch onto when your dog barks back at you. Give it a sharp tug when he sasses you and tell him firmly, "No. Stop that."

Don't allow demanding behaviors

Jake stood beside the cupboard where the biscuits were kept, then looked expectantly toward the kitchen table, where Kathy and Roger were eating breakfast. "Bark!" he said.

Roger looked up from his coffee. "No, Jake. I'll give you a biscuit when we're done."

"Bark!" repeated Jake. "Bark! Bark!" He scampered around in circles, chasing his tail and acting silly.

Kathy laughed. "He's such a character," she said.

"Yeah, but we shouldn't give him anything until we're done," Roger said.

"Bark! Bark!" yelled Jake. He seized a plush hedgehog toy and barreled around the kitchen, nearly knocking over a plant stand.

"I'm just about done," Kathy said hastily, shoving her chair back, still chewing her toast.

"Bark!" said Jake, running toward her, still clutching his hedgehog toy.

"Okay, fine, here's your biscuit, " Kathy said crossly. "Sit. Sit down. Come on, Jake, sit!"

Jake crouched into a sort-of-sit, his hindquarters not really touching the floor, poised for take-off. As Kathy lowered her hand gingerly toward his nose, he exploded into mid-air and grabbed the biscuit, accidentally scraping her thumb with his tooth.

"Well, at least he sat," Kathy said with a sigh.

When you allow your dog to be demanding, he doesn't conclude that you are a wonderful person.

He concludes that you are lower in the pecking order than he had thought—which makes **him** HIGHER than he had thought!

 Granting one demanding behavior, however innocent it may seem, usually leads to another demanding behavior.

Why? Because a dog is compelled by his instincts to grab the inch you offer and see if he can make it a foot. In this way, he tests his position in the pecking order to see if he can advance himself.

Your answer must be NO.

Note that your dog doesn't actually have to GET the biscuit in order to be demanding.

It's the very act of barking or whining at you, or poking you with his nose or paw, that is demanding.

It goes without saying that you should not give your dog a treat when he demands it so rudely. But just as importantly you need to let him know that the demanding behaviors themselves are unacceptable.

Tell him firmly, "No. Stop that." If he persists, put him in his crate for a 15-minute Time Out.

Teach your dog when "Enough is Enough"

Word #10: "Enough"

"Jake, stop pestering me!" Kathy was sitting on the sofa trying to read. She had been petting him, but after awhile she just wanted to read. Jake was having none of that. He kept shouldering himself between her knees and wedging his head into her lap. Kathy kept pushing him away, but he only wagged his tail and came charging right back.

This is what can happen if you pet your dog too much, hold your dog too much, or sit on the couch absently stroking your dog every time you watch TV or read a book.

You may be creating an unhealthy dependency.

Some dependent dogs become jealous toward other people or other pets, because they don't like you giving your attention to anyone else.

Some dependent dogs get so accustomed to your fondling and cuddling that when you take your hand away or go out for the day, they become angry and sulky. They may act out their feelings by barking persistently, or by digging holes, or by having housebreaking "accidents," or by destroying something.

Some dependent dogs become nervous and insecure about facing the world without your hand on their back. When you're gone, their separation anxiety may drive them to misbehavior—and such dependency, of course, is terrible for their mental and emotional health.

There are two lessons to be learned here:

1. Don't pet your dog too much.
2. YOU decide when to stop.

How to teach your dog healthy independence

When you sit on the couch with your dog, pet him for no more than a minute or two. Then tell him, "Good boy. That's enough." and take your hand away.

If he nudges for more, put him on the floor and tell him firmly, "No. Stop that. Enough." Say "ee-NUFF" with emphasis. Go on watching TV. It's up to him to find something else to do.

If he still persists in seeking attention, put him in his crate for 15 minutes. Don't pet him or speak to him as you do so. Simply lead him to his crate, place him inside, and close the door.

"What if my dog nudges me when I haven't been petting him?"

Every dog occasionally solicits petting by climbing onto your lap or nudging your hand. This is normal. But when it happens frequently and your dog won't stop, it has crossed the line to demanding/dependency.

Take control of his soliciting behavior

1. Pull your hands back. Put them behind your back if necessary. If you push your dog away, you're putting your hands on him—which is exactly what he wants.

2. Tell your dog to sit. (We'll cover the Sit command shortly.) When he sits, pet him for about ten seconds.

    Thus, petting becomes his reward for following YOUR command, rather than your following HIS command of "Nudge nudge, I insist that you pet me right now."

3. After the ten seconds of petting, tell him, "Good boy. Enough." If he keeps trying to solicit more, put him in his crate for 15 minutes.

Build routines for your dog

Each morning, as my husband walks down the porch steps on his way to work, I stand at the door holding our dog Buffy so she can watch him leave. "Bye-Bye, Daddy!" I call. It's for Buffy's benefit rather than my husband's. He's getting into his car and can't hear me.

My consistent use of "Bye-Bye!" has led to Buffy's understanding that Daddy leaves in the morning and returns later. (At least we assume that's her understanding! No one can really get into a dog's head and know for sure.) But I believe that in her mind, "Bye-Bye" has come to mean temporary separation and it's a familiar phrase that she now expects as part of her normal day.

Our human world is so complicated for your dog to understand that it's important to build predictable, familiar routines onto which he can "hang his hat."

- Routines reassure your dog that, regardless of the confusion going on in the hectic world of human beings, everything in HIS little world is predictable.
- Routines reassure him that he knows what comes next—that he knows what "this" event signifies, that he knows what "that" event signifies.
- Routines reassure him that his world is the same as it was yesterday and will probably be the same tomorrow.
- Routines reassure him that YOU are dependable, that he can count on you to say and do things that he understands.

> As much as possible, structure your dog's life around routines. Do the same things in the same order—and most importantly, use the same words.

Speak well of your dog

When Roger welcomes guests into his house, he always points at his dog Jake, who is invariably bounding around the room, barking with wild abandon. "That's Jake," Roger says. "Also known as Pinhead. What a numbskull! Even flunked obedience school!" His guests always chuckle and look upon Jake with good-natured pity.

If your dog's name or nickname is Dumbo or Bonkers, you probably don't think much of his mental abilities. You probably don't ask much of him, either.

The problem is that your dog can tell that you don't think much of his abilities—and he will live up to those expectations. Your low opinion and minimal expectations are actually contributing to his "dumb" behavior.

Change his name or nickname, and you'll change your expectations of him. Then when you start requiring more from him, he will change his behavior accordingly.

The same with names like Trouble. Or Devil. Or Killer. If you expect your dog to be mischievous, aggressive, or stupid, it comes through in your voice, in your facial expressions, in your body language. And your dog is likely to give you exactly what you expect.

I recommend using complimentary, optimistic names and nicknames for your dog that suggest intelligence and good nature.

If you've already named your dog something less than complimentary, you can still change his name. Many people who adopt a dog change his name. A more flattering name (or at least nickname) can start your new relationship off in a better direction.

Chapter 8
Crate Training

Eight reasons your dog needs a crate

I mentioned crates when I advised putting your dog in his crate for a Time Out after misbehavior.

A crate is a plastic or wire cage, large enough inside for your dog to stand up, turn around, and lie down comfortably to sleep.

Every dog should have a crate.

A crate is a "den"—a place of security for your dog

Just as children love to tuck themselves into clubhouses, dogs love to take refuge in small enclosed darkened areas. In a corner, under a table, behind the recliner, under blankets. By giving your dog a sanctuary all his own, you help him feel safe and secure.

A crate is an aid for housebreaking

Your dog's natural instincts are to not soil his sleeping quarters.

A crate prevents mischief

Dogs are driven by instinct and curiosity to learn about their surroundings, and they learn with their mouths—picking up, chewing, and/or swallowing anything that isn't nailed down, and some things that are! The instincts to chew are strongest during the puppy/teenage months—two to eighteen months of age.

These are natural instincts, but if left unchecked, they will become bad habits and will be difficult to break later. Not to mention the damage done to your home and belongings, and the risk of your puppy getting into something that could poison or choke him.

> You can prevent these bad habits from developing—and protect your puppy's life—by crating him whenever you leave the house for a couple of hours. (But NOT if you need to be gone longer than that—dogs should NOT be left in a crate if you're gone all day!)

A crate makes a great nighttime bed

When your dog is sleeping safely in his crate, you don't have to worry about what else he might be doing all night. Eventually you'll be able to leave the crate door open or remove it entirely, and he will continue to go into his crate, on his own, for sleeping at night.

 "Can't my dog sleep in my bed with me?"

In most cases, this isn't a good idea. There are four reasons why I recommend that your dog not sleep with you:

1. A dog who sleeps in your bed may end up viewing himself as an equal to you, like the two of you are littermates. Not a good lesson for a follower dog to learn.
2. When a dog sleeps in your bed, you may find yourself taking great pains not to disturb him. If you start to roll over and your dog groans or opens one eye and you stop moving, he may learn that he can prevent you from "inconveniencing" him. Not a good lesson for a follower dog to learn.
3. Some dogs will begin grumbling or even growling if you accidentally bump them or disturb them while they're sleeping. Not a good habit for a follower dog to develop.
4. Finally, if you're married or otherwise partnered, a dog in your bed may position himself, deliberately or accidentally, between you and your significant other. Um...that's bad.

> So unless you're single, with a large bed and an already well-behaved dog with no behavior problems, your dog should sleep in a separate bed, although IN your bedroom is okay, if you both you and partner agree.

A crate protects your dog in the car

You and your children are buckled in—so too should your dog be, either wearing a harness that's attached to the seatbelt in the back seat, or riding inside a crate that's buckled into the back seat.

A crate makes your dog a good visitor

When you're in a strange place, your dog may not behave as reliably as he normally does. You don't want him having an accident or getting into mischief in someone else's home or in a motel. Bringing a crate along when you're traveling or visiting friends shows courtesy and respect for your host.

A crate confines your dog for short periods

For example, when you're washing the floor. When you have guests over who are allergic to (or uncomfortable around) dogs. When your dog is sick or injured and needs to have his movements restricted. When you have multiple dogs and you need to do something with one dog while the other one stays out of the way.

 There will be plenty of times when you need your dog to be safely confined. Then you'll be glad you have a crate.

Your dog will have to stay in a crate at the vet's or groomer's

A dog who is already accustomed to a crate will be much less stressed when he has to stay temporarily in one elsewhere. As our dog's guardians, it's our responsibility to prepare him for the real world so he's not frightened by normal things that happen to him.

Plastic crates versus wire crates

What I like about plastic crates

Compared to wire-mesh crates, plastic crates have a cozier, den-like atmosphere, which most dogs prefer.

Plastic crates restrict your dog's view of his surroundings, making him more likely to curl up and go to sleep.

Plastic crates are warmer than wire crates. In cold climates, if you turn your heat down at night, your dog will be more snug and comfy in a plastic crate. This is especially appreciated by toy breeds and shorthaired breeds.

Plastic crates come in pastel colors and look less "kennel-ish" than wire crates.

What I don't like about plastic crates

Compared to wire crates, plastic crates are more difficult to clean. With no removable pan, if your dog goes to the bathroom in the crate, you have to reach all the way inside to clean it. Yuck.

In hot climates, if you don't have air conditioning, plastic crates are stuffier than wire crates. This can be uncomfortable for dogs with thick or heavy coats and it can be downright dangerous for dogs with short faces who don't breathe well even in normal temperatures.

> When I'm buying a plastic crate, I look for the Pet Porter or Vari-Kennel brands, both made by Doskocil. Compared to other brands, I find them more durable, easier to open, and more secure when closed.

What I like about wire crates

Wire crates come in collapsible models that can be folded and stashed in your closet or in the trunk of your car.

Wire crates have removable pans that slide out for quick and easy cleaning.

Wire crates allow more air circulation in hot stuffy weather, a boon if you don't have air conditioning, especially for dogs with heavy coats or short faces.

What I don't like about wire crates

Their openness doesn't create that secure den atmosphere that most dogs prefer. However, you can create that feeling yourself by draping a towel or sheet over the top, back, and sides. Tuck the ends of the towel under the crate so your dog can't pull it inside to chew on it.

Wire crates are not very elegant-looking. They can't help but look like kennels.

Wire crates clink and rattle when your dog moves around in them.

> 💡 I don't use wire crates any more, but when I did, I preferred the Midwest brand, which is sturdy and reasonably priced.

How large the crate should be

A crate should be:

- tall enough for your dog to stand up in
- wide enough for him to be able to turn around in
- deep enough so he can lie down with his front paws stretched comfortably in front of him, i.e. he shouldn't have to curl up in a ball to fit in the crate

Now, if you've acquired a breed of puppy that will be much larger as an adult, then buying an adult-sized crate NOW means he will have a huge area to sleep in. Too huge, in fact, because your puppy will likely sleep in one half of the crate and go to the bathroom in the other half. Not very desirable, don't you agree?

There are two solutions:

1. Go ahead and buy an adult-sized crate and make it fit his current puppy dimensions by walling off the back section with a **divider** that you make out of wood or metal or plastic.
2. Buy a smaller crate NOW for housebreaking, and buy a larger crate later to fit his adult size.

Where to put the crate

Put the crate where there is family activity going on—typically the kitchen, living room, or family room.

Don't put the crate in an isolated area such as the basement, utility room, or garage.

Crates don't need to be stuck out in the open. With a little thought, you can incorporate a small crate into your decor by fitting it under an end table, tucking it into a corner of the room, and/or camouflaging it with silk greenery.

Other tips on locating the crate

- If your dog isn't housebroken yet, try to locate the crate near the door that leads to the back yard. The shorter the distance, the less likely he will have accidents between the crate and the door when you let him out of the crate and he really has to go.
- Don't place the crate where the sun can shine directly on it.
- Don't place the crate where a heating/cooling register, fan, or air conditioner can blow on it. **Drafts are very bad for dogs!**

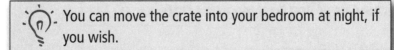 You can move the crate into your bedroom at night, if you wish.

What to put inside the crate

If your dog is housebroken

Place a thick towel, blanket, or sheepskin pad inside the crate. Remove any labels and fringes so your dog can't chew on them. Or you can buy a specialized crate pad made of foam with a slick vinyl cover. I don't particularly like these because the cover is prone to staining and is hard to take off (for washing) and even harder to put back on. And if urine somehow leaks through the vinyl to the foam pad beneath, it can really stink.

If your dog is not housebroken

Put newspapers in the crate. You can add a towel on top of the newspapers, but it shouldn't be too thick and absorbent—because if your dog pees in his crate, you actually WANT him to be a little uncomfortable on wet bedding. It's a subtle motivator for him to keep his crate clean.

> Don't put so-called "housebreaking pads" in the crate. Don't use them elsewhere, either. They encourage your dog to go to the bathroom indoors—which is a tough habit to break later on.

 Don't put a water bowl in the crate. It will spill, or your dog will splash in it and make a mess. And drinking too much water just makes him need to go out more. Makes sense, yes?

Teaching your dog to sleep in his crate

Word #11: "Go Crate"

Some trainers will tell you to wait for your dog to go into the crate on his own. Encourage him to go in, they say, by putting his food dish inside the crate, or by tossing a toy or treat inside—but don't force him to go in.

Now, if you have an adult Great Dane, I agree. But with a puppy of any breed, or a smallish adult, I prefer the direct approach.

Provide your dog with some brisk play or exercise before his first crating experience. If he's tired, he's more likely to nap when he goes into the crate.

When you're ready, lead him (or carry him, if he's very small) to the crate. Don't call him with a "Come" command! You don't want him to associate "Come" with an experience that he may not like at first.

Don't worry, your dog will come to love the security of his crate. But in the beginning, when it's **your** idea—and then you close the door—he may consider the whole experience a bummer. So don't call him.

When you arrive at the crate, say in a happy voice, "Go crate!" Place him inside, praise him cheerfully, and give him a quick treat (for example, a tiny biscuit or piece of cooked chicken), plus a Nylabone® chew toy. (We'll talk more about toys later in this book.) Close the crate door and sit down in a chair across the room to read a book.

Expect protesting. Ignore it. It should subside within a few minutes when your dog realizes that it's not working and that he might as well chew on his bone or drift off to sleep.

As soon as your dog is quiet, wait five more minutes. In other words, he must go five minutes straight without barking or whining before you let him out.

The right way to let your dog out of his crate

Word #12: "Okay!"

The way you release your dog from his crate is very important. If you rush toward the crate, fling open the door, and welcome him out like a released prisoner ("Yay! You're free!"), then the next time you put him in the crate he won't be able to relax. He will be "wired" the whole time, just itching to be released from exile.

So when you release him, do it in a low-key, matter-of-fact way.

1. Walk casually toward the crate.
2. Open the crate door and say, in a quiet voice, "Okay, Jake."
3. When he comes out, don't touch him. Don't pet or play with him. Just say simply, "Do you need to go OUT?" (We'll be teaching this phrase very soon!)
4. Take him outside to his potty area.

> Yes, even if he has only been confined for five minutes. You want to establish the habit that after being in the crate, he will always be able to go outside. This routine will help him to "hold it" while he's in the crate.

How to handle barking or whining in the crate

If a full 30 minutes goes by and your dog still hasn't settled down for his five minutes of quiet time—in other words, if he has barked or whined for virtually the entire time—it's time for a correction. (Although if you have close neighbors, you shouldn't wait 30 minutes—do it sooner!)

First, try correcting him from a distance. For example, you might fire a well-aimed spray of water from a squirt gun or spray bottle. Tell him "No" at the same time.

Other options include shaking a metal can full of coins, beeping the handheld Barker Breaker® I told you about in Chapter 3, or whacking a fly swatter against the wall or coffee table.

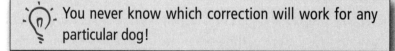

> You never know which correction will work for any particular dog!

Whichever one you try, stop it the instant your dog stops barking or whining. The lesson should be that his own barking causes a spray of water or a loud startling sound—and that his silence stops it.

If corrections from a distance fail, thwack the fly swatter directly against the crate or give the crate a mild shake, along with a firm "No. Stop that."

> Under no circumstances—well, okay, if your house is on fire!—should you remove your dog from his crate at any time when he is actually barking or whining, or immediately after he has barked or whined. Don't even remove him to CORRECT him.

Many dogs, you see, are perfectly willing to take a correction if it includes getting out of the crate. Make sure every family member understands that your dog must never be let out of the crate during (or immediately after) barking or whining. If you let him out, you are training him to bark and whine whenever he wants out.

Teaching your dog to go into his crate

After you've lead or carried him to his crate many, many times, he will have heard the phrase "Go crate!" many, many times.

The next step is to get him to go into his crate when you tell him to—without needing to lead him or carry him.

1. Wait for a time when you are both in the same room as the crate. Choose a moment when he is looking at you. Gesture toward the crate and say cheerfully, "Jake, go crate!" Your voice should be happy and excited.
2. Walk toward the crate, patting your hands together to encourage him to follow you. If necessary, take his collar and lead him toward the crate, repeating cheerfully, "Go crate! Good boy!"

3. At the door to the crate, take your hand off his collar and encourage him to go in. A strategic nudge or motivating him with a treat may be necessary.

4. As soon as he's inside, praise him. "Yay! Good crate!" Give him the treat. Close the door. When he's been quiet in there for a minute, open the door and release him with "Okay."

> Remember to be very casual about releasing him from the crate. You want him to be excited about going INTO the crate—not hyped about coming out!

5. Once he has come out, let him wander around for awhile, then send him back into the crate. Do this routine three times—no more. Then take him outside for his potty break.

Now it's simply a matter of repetition and persistence. Eventually you should be able to send him to his crate from a different room. Follow behind him to make sure he ends up in his crate.

> **As with all vocabulary words,**
> **never tell him to "Go crate!"**
> **without making absolutely sure**
> **that he does so.**

Dogs love patterns and routines. If you always send your dog to his crate immediately before or after a certain event, such as supper or bedtime or when you pick up your car keys, he may begin heading for his crate as soon as he observes the "triggering" event.

My dog Buffy is fabulous at learning patterns. When I was teaching her to go into her crate, I would say, in a teasing voice, "Guess where YOU have to go?" just before I said, "Go crate."

Well, it wasn't long before all I had to say was, "Guess where YOU have to go?" and she would make a beeline for her crate. Guests get a kick out of it!

If your dog hates his crate

What if your dog really IS an adult Great Dane? Or what if he's a smaller dog who resists going into the crate so forcefully that it's just too difficult for you to physically make him do it?

Then you'll have to move more slowly.

1. Place the crate near your dog's favorite sleeping area. Inside the crate, put a thick blanket with his scent (or your scent) on it. In other words, not a freshly-washed blanket with no scent. You want the crate to smell homey and familiar.

2. At mealtime, put his food bowl inside the crate. Place it just inside the door where he can see it. Make sure the door is propped open so it can't accidentally close on him.

   He'll soon realize that he has to stick his head into the crate to eat. Over some period of days, depending on his degree of reluctance, slide the bowl further back in the crate until finally he must enter the crate to eat.

3. At some point when he is doing well, close the door. If he accepts this calmly, let him stay in the crate for only a minute or two before you open the door and let him out.

   However, if he protests, you'll have to wait until he stops barking or whining before you let him out.

> Whenever your dog is not in his crate, leave the crate door open so he can go in if he wants. Praise him whenever he does go in of his own accord. Occasionally give him a treat inside the crate.

If you work all day...can your dog stay in a crate?

Absolutely not. Don't leave your dog in a crate for more than four hours during the day.

"But he sleeps in there all night!" you protest. Yes, nighttime is different. When your dog settles down to sleep at night, his entire metabolism (including his digestive system) slows down. Sleeping for eight hours in his crate at night is fine.

But after he has slept all night, he needs **activity** during the day. You can't head off to work for six or eight or ten hours each day and leave your dog in a crate. That's cruel.

 "What if I come home at lunch to let him outside?"

That's not enough.

A crate is just too small for a dog to be stuck in. Dogs are active, living creatures who need space to move around. Dogs are not hamsters or guinea pigs.

AND

Your dog would be terribly lonely. Dogs are sociable creatures—they can't be kept confined and isolated in a small space for hours, with only a brief visit or two during the day. Dogs require much more space, much more activity, and much more companionship than that.

> Sorry, but that's how it is. Dogs cannot be kept—happily—in a small confined space and without ongoing companionship.

 "So what should I do if I work all day but still want a dog?"

Honestly? You should get a different kind of pet. If you absolutely must have a dog, I recommend getting **two** dogs, who can keep each other company. They should be **adult** dogs who are already housebroken and well-behaved, so they won't need to be crated. And they should be **small** dogs who can get most of their exercise indoors.

Do not get a puppy if you work all day. Puppies require far too much attention to be left alone all day. To thrive and grow to their potential, they require mini-interactions and brief learning experiences sprinkled all throughout the day.

> Don't be tempted to get TWO puppies, either. Two mature and well-behaved **adults,** okay. But two **puppies** left alone all day just means that two of them are not getting all the attention, socialization, and training they need.

If you work all day and already HAVE a puppy

...or if you have an adolescent or adult dog who is not housebroken or is misbehaving during the day when you're gone—you're faced with a very difficult situation.

For their own safety and to keep your house intact, puppies and non-housebroken or destructive adults must be confined when you're gone.

**Yet you must NOT crate them
for more than four hours.**

The solution—which is not a great one, but may be all that's possible under these unfortunate circumstances—may be an exercise pen. An ex-pen consists of several wire panels hooked together, which you can arrange in almost any shape. Get the largest ex-pen you can find.

Or you might use a doggy gate to block off a laundry room, sun room, or kitchen.

Whatever you do, don't put your dog in a small room and close the door! Many dogs become frantic behind a closed solid door and will bark and scratch vigorously to escape.

So yes, an exercise pen or small gated-off room can work to confine your dog all day.

But it doesn't address the loneliness issue. Your poor puppy should be running around and playing during his formative months. He should be interacting with people all throughout the day. A puppy left all alone most of the day is lonely and unhappy and will never become the dog he could have been.

Chapter 9

Housebreaking

Word #13: "Do You Need to Go Out?"

If owners could choose only one skill they wanted their dog to have, *housebroken* would be very high on the list!

The two keys to housebreaking

1. Confinement—so your dog can't go to the bathroom in the wrong place.
2. Regular or constant access to the RIGHT place to "go."

Confinement means that until your dog is housebroken, he is never allowed to walk freely around the house.

Confinement means every minute of every hour of every day—unless you're sitting with your dog, playing with him, walking him, feeding him, grooming him, teaching him, or otherwise interacting with him.

> Don't allow a non-housebroken dog loose in the house when you're not watching him. Because if you take your eyes off him for just a few moments, he can go to the bathroom on your floor—and the bad habit is begun.

Regular or constant access to the RIGHT place to "go" means you let your dog outside or take him outside on a regular basis (every few hours)—or else he lets himself out through a doggy door at will. Or you can provide him with an indoor bathroom—newspapers or a litter box.

Plain and simple, those are the two keys to housebreaking.

1. If you arrange things so that the only place your dog CAN go is outside, or indoors on newspapers or in a litter box, that's the habit he will develop.
2. If, on the other hand, you give him too much freedom in the house or if you don't give him enough access to an acceptable bathroom, then he will probably "go" in the house—and that's the habit he will develop.

It's up to you!

So how do you provide both confinement and bathroom access to your dog? There are three basic methods.

Housebreaking Method #1: Crating

You will confine your dog in a crate, and you will take him outside regularly so he can go to the bathroom.

This is the most common method of housebreaking. Whenever you're not interacting directly with your dog, he is safe in his crate.

In lieu of leaving him in the crate, you can tie his leash to your belt so that he accompanies you around the house, at least for part of the day. Just keep an eagle eye on him so he doesn't pee on the floor right at your feet!

On a regular basis throughout the day, you take him outside to a specific potty area to go to the bathroom.

Step-by-step housebreaking using the crate method

Establish a regular feeding schedule, so your dog's digestive cycle will be predictable. Every dog is different in how quickly he digests food and therefore how soon he needs to "go" after a meal.

Generally, puppies under four months old need to eat four times a day. Between four and six months, you can drop to three meals a day, and between six and eight months, two meals a day. (These are just rough guidelines—your dog's mileage may vary!)

> Do NOT leave food down all the time for your dog to nibble at. It makes housebreaking too difficult. In addition, your dog's appetite is a good barometer of his health and it's easier to keep tabs on his appetite when you're offering him regularly spaced meals.

Establish a regular in-and-out schedule. In the beginning, try to take him outside about every two hours.

Start with first thing in the morning. Then whenever he wakes from a nap. Immediately after he eats or drinks. Immediately after play periods. Whenever he suddenly sniffs the floor or begins walking in circles. And last thing at night.

When it's time to go outside, ask him in a bright voice, "Do you need to go OUT?"

Snap his leash on quickly. Tell him cheerfully, "Go OUT! OUTside!" and head briskly for the door. Try to use the same door every time.

Choose a potty area. It should be the same spot every time, though you may have to experiment to find out where your dog "goes" best.

- Some dogs prefer grass, whereas other dogs hate grass, especially in wet weather, or when the grass is too deep, or when it's too short and prickly. Some dogs get so preoccupied sniffing all the scents on grass that they can't focus on doing their business. Find another potty area for sniffy dogs!
- Some dogs prefer dirt. Some like gravel.
- Some dogs need privacy—they feel exposed out in the open and prefer to "go" behind a bush.
- Some dogs can't concentrate on their business if there's any activity going on nearby. They get distracted wanting to gawk or bark. These dogs need a quiet, boring spot.
- Some submissive dogs are too intimidated to "go" if they can see another dog or hear another dog barking in the distance.
- Male dogs who lift their leg need a vertical object to pee against.

Take your dog directly to his potty area, on leash. Encourage him, in a pleasant voice, "Hurry up" or "Go potty." But don't sound stern or commanding. Your dog needs to feel relaxed in order to be able to go!

Now...stand still. Ignore your dog entirely—except for watching him out of the corner of your eye. Do NOT make eye contact with him or he will pay attention to you instead of concentrating on doing his business. Don't say anything to him. Talking will only distract him.

If he just stands there or sits or lies down, take a few steps in one direction or another to get him moving, then stand still again. Your dog can circle around you, so there are plenty of spots he can "go" within the length of the leash. If you walk around too much, he will come to look at these outings as walks rather than dedicated bathroom breaks.

Keep an eye on your watch. Allow your dog about 5 minutes. If he hasn't gone by then, bring him back inside and put him in his crate.

Go about your business elsewhere in the house. In ten or fifteen minutes, take him back outside. From your persistence he will learn that he must go to the bathroom—even a token drop or two—before he is allowed to run and play.

When he finally does go, make a big deal out of it! "Yay! Good boy!" Give him a treat. Then romp and play with him before bringing him back inside. Or bring him inside and play with him indoors.

Then, unless you're going to groom him, or sit with him on the couch, or teach him a new word, or take him for a walk, or whatever, he goes back into his crate. Confinement, remember!

Housebreaking Method #2: Exercise Pen/Newspapers

If you're gone more than four hours a day, your puppy needs constant access to a bathroom spot. You can lay down newspapers on the floor and surround them with an exercise pen. That's where your puppy should stay whenever you're not interacting with him.

Step-by-step housebreaking using the newspapers method

1. Shape the exercise pen tightly around the newspapers so the papers fill all of the pen except for a small blanket or bed, food and water bowls, and a toy. Leave no open space. Few dogs want to soil their blanket, so they will almost always go on the papers if you give them no other choice. This builds the correct habit from day one.

2. Place your dog on his blanket in the pen. As you did when crate-training, you should expect some initial noisemaking. If the barking or whining doesn't subside within a short time, correct it.

3. Whenever you see your dog use the papers, praise him lavishly. After he has been using the papers reliably for several days, slowly expand the size of the pen (or reduce the area of papers covering the floor) so he has some room to play that's not on the papers.

If he makes a mistake by "going" on the now open floor inside the pen, rather than on the papers, reduce the pen again so that he must go on the papers. Then give him another few days of practice before you try again to expand the open area and reduce the papered area.

> Remember, your puppy should only be outside the pen when you're interacting with him or when his leash is tied to your belt so that he must follow you around.

Housebreaking Method #3: Litter Box

A litter box appeals to many people because it looks tidier than newspapers and is easier to clean.

However, many dogs don't like to limit their elimination to such a small area as a litter box. If you've ever watched a dog looking for just the right bathroom spot, you know how they like to wander around in circles!

> Litter boxes work best for tiny dogs such as Chihuahuas, Maltese, and Yorkies. And even then, the bigger the box, the better.

A regular cat box is too shallow for dogs, who tend to back up to the edge and leave their "deposits" on or over the side. You may need to make your own box from a clear plastic storage bin with high sides. Cut a squared-off U-shape in one side to make a step-over entrance, leaving enough of the box below the entrance to hold the litter in the box.

Litter boxes work better for females, because males who lift their leg can spray urine everywhere. With males, the box needs extra-high sides. Some people build a very large litter box and include a vertical "pee pole" covered with plastic. Yes, really!

Warning: Don't use "clumping" kitty litter!

So-called "clumping" litter hardens into a tight compact little ball when it gets wet, i.e. when urine soaks into it. When clumping litter first hit the market, it seemed like a dream come true because it was so easy to scoop up and much less wasteful of litter.

But most conveniences come with a price, and we now know that when a dog or cat licks clumping litter off his paws or coat and swallows it, the litter gets WET (from his saliva and stomach fluid) and then guess what?

It clumps in his stomach—and now Doggy or Kitty are in serious trouble.

You can find out more about the dangers of clumping kitty litter by doing a Google™ search. Or start with this web site: *www.thelighthouseonline.com/catmomtoc.html*

So what kind of litter should you use? For both dogs and cats, use litter made from recycled newspaper. Good brands include Second Nature and Yesterday's News. These litters are non-toxic, dust-free, super-absorbent, and environmentally-friendly. You can buy them at pet stores such as PetsMart and at health food stores.

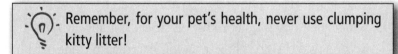

Remember, for your pet's health, never use clumping kitty litter!

Step-by-step housebreaking using the litter box method

Word #14: "Go Box"

1. Shape your exercise pen tightly around the litter box so that the box fills all of the pen except for a small blanket or bed, food and water bowls, and a toy. Leave no open space. Few dogs want to soil their blanket, so they will almost always go in the box if you give them no other choice. This builds the correct habit from day one.

2. Place your dog on his bed in the pen. As you did when crate-training, you should expect some initial noisemaking. If the barking or whining doesn't subside within a short time, correct it.

3. Once your dog is quiet in his pen, occasionally encourage him to step into the litter box by holding a treat in front of his nose and leading him in. Tell him, "Go box!" as you do so. Give him the treat once he's inside.

4. Whenever you see him step into the box on his own, even to play, praise him. If you actually see him go to the bathroom in there, praise him lavishly and give him a treat!

5. After he has been using the box reliably for a week or so, slowly expand the size of the pen so he has some room to play.

    If at any time he makes a mistake by "going" on the now open floor inside the pen, rather than in his box, reduce the pen again so that he must go in the box. Then give him another few days of practice before you expand the pen again.

6. Remember, he should only be outside the pen when you're interacting with him or when his leash is tied to your belt so that he must follow you around. Occasionally use a treat to lead him back into the pen and box so that he will remember where it is and have pleasant associations with it.

Housebreaking Method #4: Doggy Door

In my house, we have a small mud room off the kitchen. In the mud room is a doggy door leading outside to a small fenced "potty" yard.

When we were housebreaking our dog Buffy, we put a gate between the mud room and the kitchen so that Buffy was confined to the mud room, where she had access to the potty yard via the doggy door.

Caution: The Doggy Door method of confinement and bathroom access should only be considered if your dog **doesn't bark** when he goes outside. Nothing is more annoying to neighbors than a dog who can go outside at will and bark!

Step-by-step housebreaking using the doggy door method

1. Confine your dog in the small gated room whenever you're not interacting with him.
2. For the first few days, remove the heavy flap on the doggy door (or tie the flap up out of the way) so that your dog has free access through the hole into his potty yard.

   If he is reluctant to go through the hole at first, someone should stand inside the room with him while someone else stands outside in the potty yard, crouched near the open hole. Take turns waving treats through the hole and calling him. You should soon have him running in and out through the open door.
3. Once he has the hang of the open hole, you may want to hang a light towel or cotton cloth over the opening for a few more days, as a gradual transition toward the heavier vinyl flap. Use the treats to teach him that he can push through the cloth and that he only has to poke his nose through it or under it in order to scramble through.

   Eventually you'll move on to the heavier flap. Though it looks daunting at first, rest assured that even toy dogs can move it.
4. Periodically throughout the day, go into the little gated room and ask your dog, "Do you need to go OUT? Go OUT!" Use hand motions to encourage him to do so. If necessary, lead him

to and through the doggy door by the collar. You go outside, too, and put something across the doggy door, just temporarily, so he can't run right back in.

Don't block the door on the **inside**, or else he might rush through the flap and ram his head into the barrier!

5. Pick a spot to stand where you can observe your dog, but don't interact with him. Let him go about his business, which hopefully will include going to the bathroom.

> Do you see the advantage of separating the potty yard from the main yard—and making it small? If your dog can run around a big yard, he will want to play and explore rather than focus on doing his business.

6. After five minutes, if your dog hasn't gone to the bathroom, remove the barrier so he can go back inside the house if he wants to. You can return to the house, too, and go about your own business for ten or fifteen minutes. Then try again.

7. When he finally does go to the bathroom in the yard, make a big deal out it! "Yay! Good boy!" Give him a treat. Then let him out of the potty yard and romp and play with him for awhile, either outdoors in the big yard, or in the house, before returning him to his gated room.

In this way, he will learn that he must go to the bathroom—even a token drop or two—before you will run and play with him.

Housebreaking accidents

If your dog goes to the bathroom on the floor of your house, here's what to do:

1. Correct him.
   - Get hold of his collar.
   - Take him to the accident.
   - Pull his head down near the accident—**but not touching it!** Just close enough so he can see it.
   - Tell him firmly, "No. Bad."

This is a mild correction, because it is YOUR fault that your dog erred. If you had been watching him closely enough during this critical housebreaking phase, this should not have happened. Every accident in the house is a step backward in housebreaking. Don't let accidents happen!

2. Take him to his proper bathroom spot.
   - If it's outside and you usually take him there personally, then quickly snap on his leash, tell him, "Go out!" and take him out.
   - If he uses a doggy door to get there, tell him, "Go out!" and escort him to the doggy door. Make sure he goes through it.
   - If his bathroom spot is a litter box, tell him, "Go box!" and take him there.

> Of course, immediately after an accident, most dogs will not need to go again. So this trip to the correct spot will probably be unproductive. Doesn't matter. The point is to remind him where you want him to go.

3. Put him in his crate for a 15-minute Time Out.
   The Time Out will give you a chance to…

4. Clean up the mess.

   Soap and water are not enough. Detergents will clean the stain, but they won't get rid of the microscopic odor particles that will attract your dog back to the soiled area.

   Ammonia-based household cleaners are the worst of all. Urine contains ammonia, so your dog is **attracted** to ammonia products. That's not what you want!

   White vinegar mixed with water does a decent job of neutralizing odors, but the best type of cleaner is an **enzymatic cleaner** that actually breaks down (eats) microscopic odor particles. My favorite enzymatic cleaner is Nature's Miracle®, which you can find at PetsMart and other pet supply stores.

How long it takes to housebreak a dog

Some dogs catch on to the concept in a week. Some dogs take several weeks. Some dogs don't get it for many months.

Just keep in mind that **understanding** the concept of housebreaking is only the first step to actual, honest-to-goodness housebreaking. The second step is for your dog to be able to do it.

Up until four to six months old, puppies can't last longer than two to four hours during the day without eliminating. Their bladder and digestive system are simply not developed enough to "hold it" longer than that.

> In other words, if you acquire an eight-week-old puppy, you're going to need to be patient for several MONTHS while your infant's internal organs develop.

Adult dogs over a year old may be able to go eight hours during the day without eliminating. However, many perfectly normal adults can only go about six hours. You have to learn and accept the limitations of your own individual dog.

But let me ask you this:

How long are YOU comfortable holding it? Don't you usually visit the bathroom at least once during the day?

Well, your dog should be granted the same courtesy! Even if he can physically hold it for eight hours during the day, he shouldn't have to—day after day. It's cruel.

In fact, some breeds are prone to developing urinary infections and kidney stones when they're forced to retain their urine all day.

Night time is different. At night your dog's metabolism, including his digestive system, slows down. Most adult dogs (and many puppies) can sleep eight hours through the night, without needing to go.

The hardest breeds to housebreak

Here are some of the hardest breeds to housebreak (listed in alphabetical order, not order of difficulty!):

Affenpinscher	Italian Greyhound
Basset Hound	Japanese Chin
Beagle	Maltese
Bichon Frise	Miniature Pinscher
Boston Terrier	Pekingese
Brussels Griffon	Pomeranian
Chihuahua	Pug
Chinese Crested	Shih Tzu
Dachshund	Silky Terrier
French Bulldog	Yorkshire Terrier

Toy dogs dominate the list because owners often buy them for the express purpose of "spoiling" and so they're reluctant to crate them. ("Little Snookums would be so unhappy!")

The problem is, when a toy dog is loose in the house, he finds it so easy to sneak behind a chair or under the coffee table, where it takes only a few seconds for the deed to be done. The result is hard to see and often goes undiscovered for weeks. By then the bad habit is entrenched.

But even when properly crate-trained, toy breeds often take much longer to housebreak. The reality is that tiny dogs are not natural creatures and that artificially manipulating their genes to shrink their structure may also affect the integrity of their internal organs.

So expect more problems with tiny dogs. Be extra-vigilant about confining them—some toys are not ready for freedom in the house until eight or ten months old!

When to let your dog loose in the house

Gradually. Your dog needs hundreds of experiences "going" in the correct bathroom spot in order to build the right habit. If you grant freedom too soon, a sudden string of accidents can set housebreaking back in a hurry.

If you've been working on housebreaking for at least a month AND your dog seems to have the hang of it AND he is at least five or six months old...

during a time when you're reading a book or working on your computer...

when you normally would have had your dog in his crate...

let him loose in the room with you.

But take precautions:

- Close the door so he can't wander elsewhere.
- While you're working, look up frequently to see how he's doing.

After an hour, take him outside. If he goes to the bathroom when you take him out, praise him lavishly and give him another period of freedom in the same room. Whereas if he doesn't go, put him in his crate for awhile, then try him outside again. Once he's successfully gone outside, give him another period of freedom in the room with you.

> As you can see, you don't throw your house open to him all at once. One room at a time. One hour at a time. And if he has an accident when you're giving him more freedom, go back to crating for awhile.

Problem: soiling the crate

If your dog is going to the bathroom inside his crate, re-read the section on crate training. Be sure you're following the step-by-step instructions. Once you're sure you're doing everything right...

Make sure the crate is small enough that your dog can't sleep in one end and go to the bathroom in the other. Use a smaller crate, or put in a divider.

Make sure you're not crating your dog longer than he can physically hold it. He should not be crated for more than four hours during the day. (A puppy can't hold it for more than TWO hours.)

Make sure he has had a chance to go to the bathroom before you put him in the crate.

Make sure he hasn't drunk a lot of water just before being crated. And there should be no food or water in the crate.

Make sure the bedding material is not too soft and plush, else it will absorb urine and allow him to sleep in comfort after he pees. If he does "go" in his crate, you want him to be just a little uncomfortable!

Have your vet test for a urinary infection that might be making your poor dog need to go more often.

Make sure you have worked out a reasonable eating and elimination schedule.

For example, my dog Buffy goes outside to the bathroom at 7 a.m.. She eats breakfast at 9 a.m. and goes outside through her doggy door at various times during the day. She eats supper at 9:30 p.m., goes out for the last time around 10 p.m., then sleeps all night. You and your dog will need to work out your own best schedule—but there does need to be one.

If your dog is having difficulty making it through the night, move the crate into your bedroom. If he cries in the night, take him outside. His need to go out at night should diminish as he gets older.

Problem: marking territory (excessive leg-lifting)

Most male dogs lift their leg to urinate, but some do it too much. Excessive marking is more of a dominance issue than a housebreaking issue. A male dog lifts his leg to spray his urine as high as possible, thereby marking his territory. He's saying, "I was here! I'm one big bad dude and I claim this territory!"

Unneutered males are the worst offenders. But some neutered males do it—and some dominant **females** (whether spayed or not) do it, too.

Some breeds are much worse than others in their compulsiveness to mark territory. Toy dogs, for example, can be obsessed with marking. Some toy dogs dash around like little wind-up toys, lifting their leg busily on every vertical object larger than a blade of grass. Terriers, with their feisty personalities, can be compulsive markers, too.

Here's what to do about excessive marking

Neuter your dog. Testosterone increases dominance problems. Neutering will decrease (but not completely eliminate) your dog's testosterone levels so that he doesn't feel so compelled to be in charge.

Absolutely do not breed your dog. A male dog who has been bred is more likely to lift his leg everywhere, including inside your house.

Confine your dog. A dog who is marking in the house should not be allowed freedom in the house. Until his marking is under control, he should be out of his crate or pen only when you're interacting with him—walking him, feeding or grooming him, training him, and so on.

If you want to have him out while you're puttering around the house, tie his leash to your waist. Now he must follow you around. Both physically and psychologically, this helps establish you as the leader and him as the follower.

Clean marked areas thoroughly. Use an enzymatic cleaner. Soap and detergents don't get out the microscopic odor particles that attract your dog back to the same area. My favorite enzymatic cleaner is Nature's Miracle®.

Work hard on this 100 Words program. It will increase your dog's respect for you and make him less likely to mark. After you've taught him all of the obedience words, practice a quick succession of them, for five minutes straight, several times a day. "Heel. Sit. Stay. Come. Sit. Down." Again, this is the leader-follower scenario where you are giving commands and he is following them. Always good for building respect!

Problem: excitable/submissive urination

Urinating when excited or nervous is NOT a housebreaking problem.

Excitable urination

An excited dog, especially a young one, isn't always able to maintain control of his bladder. If he is very happy to see someone, his bladder may accidentally let go when the person reaches toward him.

Submissive urination

In the wild, a submissive canine, upon meeting a more dominant canine, crouches and releases a little urine, which is an instinctive canine signal that says to the dominant dog, "I mean no harm. I accept your superiority." A submissive dog may do the same thing when you bend over him, or reach toward him, or raise your voice. Submissive urination is most common in gentle, soft-tempered dogs such as spaniels.

> Your piddling dog is not doing this on purpose! It is an instinctive behavior that he has no control over. Corrections will only make him MORE submissive and MORE prone to piddling.

Here's how to deal with excitable or submissive urination

- When you greet an excitable or submissive dog, don't make eye contact or approach him head-on. Instead, turn your body slightly to the side so you don't look so intimidating.
- Don't lean over him or reach your hand toward him—let HIM come up to you and touch YOU when he is ready.

In other words, don't focus your attention on an excitable or submissive dog. Look past him rather than at him. It is the anticipation of being touched, or petted, or picked up, or stared at, that sets off the uncontrollable urination.

The good news is that submissive urination and excitable urination are most common in puppies and adolescents. If you don't punish the puppy for it, and if you develop his confidence in his own abilities by teaching him vocabulary words and positive behaviors, submissive or excitable urination usually (but not always, unfortunately) goes away with maturity.

Chapter 10

Handling Your Dog
(Without Getting Into World War III)

A dog who protests or grumbles or makes a fuss when you open his mouth, brush his teeth, clean his ears, clip his nails, trim his coat, brush him, or bathe him…

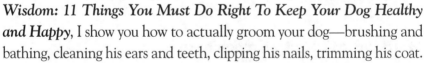

…is second-guessing your decisions about what is best for him. He is making a statement that he doesn't trust you to handle the leadership role.

In my canine health book, **Dog Care Wisdom: 11 Things You Must Do Right To Keep Your Dog Healthy and Happy,** I show you how to actually groom your dog—brushing and bathing, cleaning his ears and teeth, clipping his nails, trimming his coat.

But **Teach Your Dog 100 English Words** is about training and respect, so in this book we're going to focus on using vocabulary words that teach your dog to **accept** being handled and groomed.

Word #15: "Time For Grooming"

"Buffy! **Time for grooming!** Let's go in the basement!" Our grooming table is in the basement, you see. Try to have a specific place set aside for grooming your dog. I've guided Buffy down to the basement so many times that she knows exactly where to go. She runs downstairs and waits beside the grooming table so I can boost her up.

Sit and Stand: the basic handling positions

To teach your dog to accept handling and grooming, first choose a surface with good footing. Don't do these exercises on a slippery vinyl or wood floor!

For small dogs, a table (covered with rubber matting or toweling) is good. You have more control over your dog on a table. Just keep your hands on him so he doesn't jump or fall off.

Your goal with these exercises is to have your dog sit and stand calmly while you touch and feel all over his body.

- With puppies under four months old, it's enough to simply introduce these basic positions and accustom him to being handled. Don't be a perfectionist with young puppies!
- With dogs six months or older, you can be stricter, teaching your dog not only to accept being handled, but also to maintain each position exactly as you teach it.

Word #16: "Sit" (introduction to sit)

With your dog standing in his grooming area, say "Sit" and use your hands to place him into a sit.

Here are two methods to do that:

- One method is **Pull Up and Push Down**. With your right hand, pull up on his collar. With your left palm, push down on his hindquarters (just behind his two hipbones, or at the base of his tail). Be sure you're not pushing on his back—his spine and vertebrae are too sensitive for heavy pressure.

- Another method is **The Fold.** Place your right palm on his chest. Place your left hand (if he's small) or your left forearm (if he's larger) across his rump (below his tail and above his knees). In one smooth motion, push his chest toward his rump, while tucking his back knees forward to **fold** him into a sit over your hand or forearm.

However you accomplish it, the moment your dog is sitting, tell him "GOOD sit." This is one time when you should keep your praise quiet and calm. If you praise too enthusiastically, he will get excited and start jumping around.

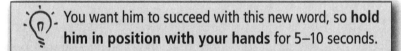

You want him to succeed with this new word, so **hold him in position with your hands** for 5–10 seconds.

Word #17: "Stand"

1. Remove your right hand from his chest and hook your fingers in his collar under his chin.
2. Quickly place your left hand, palm DOWN, under his stomach, way back in his groin area where his hindquarters are all bunched up as he sits there.
3. Draw out the word "St-aa-aa-nd" as you pull his collar gently forward with your right hand and press upward with the BACK of your left hand into your dog's lower stomach/groin area.

   Don't turn your left hand so the palm is UP. With your palm up, it's too tempting to clutch into his stomach with your fingers as you lift him up—this could startle or even hurt him. So use the BACK of your hand to raise him into a standing position.

4. Once he's standing, keep your left hand (palm down) under his stomach to prevent him from sitting. Stroke his chest with the fingers of your right hand. Praise him, "Good stand. Good stand."

5. After 5–10 seconds of standing—still holding him in position with your hands—tell him, "Sit" and guide him into a sit again.

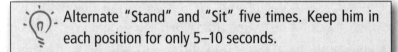 Alternate "Stand" and "Sit" five times. Keep him in each position for only 5–10 seconds.

As your dog improves

Eventually (after several days of practice), take your hands away. If he doesn't hold the sit (or stand) position when you remove your hands, say "Ah-ah" the instant he breaks position and re-place him with your hands. Be patient but persistent.

Touching your dog all over his body

When your dog is reasonably proficient at holding the Sit and Stand positions—even if you still need to steady him a bit with one hand—you can start teaching him to accept handling.

With your dog in a sitting position

1. Run your hand over his body, and your fingers through his coat.

2. Put one hand under his chin to lift his head up so you can peer into his eyes. Rub your index finger around the inner corner of his eyes, as though scraping off sleepy seeds.

3. Rub around the base of his ears. Peer inside his ears. Stroke the inside of his ears gently with your thumb.

4. Cup your hand over the top of his muzzle for a few seconds. A leader dog will occasionally rest his muzzle across the muzzle

of a follower dog, so it's good to occasionally remind your dog of the correct order of things!

Praise your dog (quietly) each time he accepts handling. If he fusses or stands up, caution him, "Ah-ah!" and scoot him (patiently) back into his Sit.

Word #18: "Open Your Mouth"

Your dog should still be sitting. Put one hand under his chin, holding his head up. Say, "OPEN your mouth. OPEN." Use the thumb of your other hand to lift up one side of his lip so you can look at his teeth.

Slide your fingers around his lips, getting him used to the odd sensation of his lips being pulled away from his teeth.

Touch his teeth, gently rubbing them with the tip of your finger. Start with his biggest teeth, the four sharp pointy "canines" (two up and two down). Move on to his incisors—the upper and lower row of small teeth across the front of his mouth. Finally, the back molars.

Word #19: "Paw"

With your dog still in his sitting position, gently tap the back of one of his front legs, down near the ankle. This will become a signal to him—a gentle tap behind a foot means you'll be lifting it up. Follow the tap by saying, "Paw" and close your hand very lightly around his ankle. Don't grasp the paw itself—you're too likely to squeeze it.

Raise his paw just a couple of inches and hold it there for just a few seconds. Praise him, "Good boy. Good paw." If he tries to pull his foot away, tell him, "Ah-ah." Make sure he remains sitting. When he has been calm for a few seconds, let go.

Repeat with his other front foot. Tap behind it. Say, "Paw" and lift it up.

Eventually (not necessarily in this first session!), move on to spreading his toes and gently rubbing a finger between them. Gently grasp each toenail, one a time, between your thumb and index finger. Fold the paw gently backward so you can touch the pads of his foot.

Now the back feet

To handle his back feet, you need to get your dog standing up, which you already know how to do: "St-aa-aa-nd."

When he's standing, tap the back of his right rear foot, say, "Paw" and close your hand lightly around his ankle. Raise his leg a couple of inches. When he accepts this calmly for a couple of seconds, let it go. Repeat with his left rear foot.

As with the front paws, eventually you want to be able to handle every part of his rear feet—including the toes, nails, and pads.

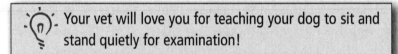 Your vet will love you for teaching your dog to sit and stand quietly for examination!

The best positions for actually grooming your dog

For brushing, I have my dog "Sit" or "Stand."
For cleaning her ears and the corners of her eyes, I have her "Sit."
For cleaning her teeth, I use "Sit" and "Open your mouth."
For clipping her nails, I use "Sit" and "Paw."

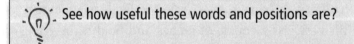 See how useful these words and positions are?

If your dog growls while being handled

Growling or snapping is a frightening sign of disrespect. A growling dog believes that he is higher in the pecking order than you are, and that you have no right to be handling him or making him do anything he doesn't want to do.

Some really spoiled dogs become positively theatrical when you try to clip their nails. Now, if you feel inclined to support other people's kids through college, you can head for the vet's office or grooming salon every couple of months simply to have your dog's nails clipped.

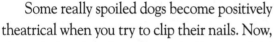 But good gosh, if your toddler threw a tantrum and wouldn't "let" you clip his fingernails, would you give in and take him to the pediatrician or beauty salon? I mean, really now!

However...a word of caution! Some common sense and judgment are required here.

If your dog is a puppy and is simply acting out with fussy growls and baby teeth, you should be able to use the respect training program presented in this book to change the pecking order in your household and bring him under your control.

But if your dog is an adult and especially if he is large and/or truly aggressive, you should call a local trainer who can schedule a few private lessons to help you control him.

Speaking for myself personally, I would not keep a dog who wouldn't "let" me clip his nails or clean his teeth. What else might such a dog decide I can't do? I would never trust him and I would never feel confident of my ability to handle him in an emergency.

Remember, my book on canine health care, **Dog Care Wisdom: 11 Things You Must Do Right To Keep Your Dog Healthy and Happy,** explains how to actually clean your dog's eyes and ears, how to brush his teeth and coat, and how to clip his nails.

The dreaded "bath" word

Word #20: "Bath"

Most dogs learn this word quickly because it's associated with such a dramatic event—being required to stand still while being doused with water and scrubbed with shampoo.

Like many children, many dogs dislike baths. So you might think that you should avoid teaching them this word because it tips them off to the upcoming event.

You're right, it does tip them off...

...but it's so funny to see my dog's melodramatic reaction when I hold up the shampoo and towel and say, "Want a BATH? Time for a BATH!"

She looks like a deer caught in the headlights. She drops her tail, lowers her body nearly to the ground, and creeps toward her crate, hoping that perhaps I'll forget what I just said.

I'm so mean!

Once in the bath, I use "Stand" rather than "Sit" because many dogs, especially smaller ones, dislike sitting in water.

Fussing in the bath should be corrected with: "Ah-ah" or "Stop that," backed up by a physical correction if necessary.

Poor behavior can be caused by poor grooming

If your dog has any behavior problems, look seriously at how he is groomed. You'd be surprised at how many behavior problems are caused or exacerbated by poor grooming.

For example, does he have hair hanging across his eyes?

A dog with hair hanging across his eyes may act nervous, timid, barky, suspicious, or aggressive—because he can't see the world clearly.

He may see only half a person walking toward him, or a disembodied arm reaching for him.

He may not be able to visually locate and identify the source of sounds, so he barks more.

He may have a short attention span because he can't focus on what you're trying to show him.

He may be physically clumsy because he can't see where he's going.

As all that hanging hair shifts and blows around in the breeze, the world appears to change right in front of his eyes. It's no wonder his behavior is unsettled!

SOLUTION:

Trim the hair short across his eyes. Yes, even if your breed is supposed to have shaggy facial hair, **trim it short.** "Show dogs" may need hair hanging across their face in order to win a ribbon, but your companion dog needs to SEE. Period.

You could lift the hair off his eyes and bunch it over his head with an elastic band or pretty bow, but then you'll never know for sure whether it's pulling on his skin and making him uncomfortable. Just **trim it short,** is my advice.

Does his coat have mats or tangles?

Mats and tangles pull on your dog's skin whenever he changes position or moves. Imagine how irritated and hypersensitive you would feel if you couldn't sit or lie down or walk in comfort.

SOLUTION:

Brush a long coat at least every other day. Especially comb through the armpits, chest, and stomach, and up inside his groin (lower belly), where painful mats often go unnoticed.

If you can't spare the time for so much brushing, **trim his coat short**. Again, it doesn't matter if his breed is "supposed" to have long hair. His comfort is more important than anything else.

> **Warning:** Some kinds of dogs should NOT be clipped short, namely "spitz type" dogs with thick double coats (like Siberian Huskies, American Eskimo Dogs, Chows, Pomeranians, etc.) If you shave or clip these coats, you can damage the hair follicles and create a chronic skin problem. More hair will fall out and the coat may not grow properly for years.

Is his skin itchy?

It's hard for an itchy dog to pay attention and learn, or even to sit still or lie down comfortably. Itchy dogs fidget!

Itchy skin can be caused by:

- Bathing too frequently.
- Bathing with the wrong shampoos.
- Not rinsing thoroughly enough.
- Fleas, allergies, and other skin conditions.
- Feeding commercial dog food—This is an often-missed but major cause of skin problems!

SOLUTION:

In my canine health book, ***Dog Care Wisdom,*** I discuss proper feeding, bathing, and flea control.

Are his toenails too long?

If your dog is reluctant to go for walks, check his toenails. It's hard to walk comfortably with long toenails! Check dewclaws, too—the extra 5th nail on the inside of your dog's ankles. Some dogs have them, and some don't. If left untrimmed, dewclaws can grow in a complete circle and pierce your dog's skin. Ouch!

Are his teeth coated with plaque or tartar?

Along with making your dog feel uncomfortable, which can cause him to act grumpy or nasty, bad teeth are a serious health hazard. Blood vessels in the gums lead straight to the heart, so minor infections in the gums can quickly become major infections in the heart.

Are his ears dirty or clogged with hair or infected?

Unhealthy ears can make any dog feel miserable and grumpy.

SOLUTION:

In my canine health book, ***Dog Care Wisdom,*** I explain how to keep your dog's nails clipped, his teeth brushed, and his ears clean and healthy.

As you can see, a poorly groomed dog is not in an ideal frame of mind for learning.

> So keep him well-groomed. If his hair, skin, toenails, eyes, ears, and teeth feel clean and comfortable, he's one more step along the road to a positive attitude and a bright, alert mind that's ready to learn.

Chapter 11

Quickly-Learned Words

Most dogs are eager for food, and any time a dog is eager for something, it's much easier to teach him the words and phrases attached to it.

"Do you want...?"

Word #21: "Are You Hungry?"
Word #22: "Want To Eat?"
Word #23: "Want Some Food?"

Ah, phrases that are music to canine ears: "Do you want...?" "Want to..." "Want some...?"

These are great phrases to teach your dog early on, because they're associated with getting something good; therefore, dogs learn them quickly. You want your dog to quickly learn the concept that sounds have meaning.

That is, dogs learn them quickly **IF you quickly provide what you're promising.**

"Jake, are you hungry?" Kathy asked. She was stirring soup on the stove for herself and Roger.

Jake cocked his head with interest and Roger picked up the dog's food bowl. Jake began dancing with excitement. "He knows his food bowl," laughed Roger. "You want to eat, huh, Jake?" Jake leaped into the air trying to grab the bowl.

"Oops, wait a minute," Roger said. "I need to go down to the basement and get a new bag of kibble." He set the bowl on the kitchen counter and headed for the basement. Jake stood uncertainly in the middle of the kitchen, looking from the food bowl to the basement stairs, his tail beginning to droop.

The minutes ticked by. "Roger!" Kathy called. Roger clumped up the basement steps, looking sheepish. "I got distracted," he said. "I saw that lamp I've been trying to fix and thought I'd check the switch again."

Kathy chuckled. "And I see you forgot the dog food. Well, our soup's ready, so Jake will have to wait until after we eat." She put Jake in the yard and they sat down to supper.

Poor Jake! Dogs live in the current moment.

Don't get your dog excited about the possibility of food, and then dilly-dally before giving it to him.

The longer the delay between the time you say a word, and the time you provide the correct object or action, the harder it will be for your dog to grasp the connection.

 You have to say a word and then IMMEDIATELY provide the correct object or action. A minute's delay is too long!

Here's the right way to turn meaningless sounds into meaningful words:

Each evening, around 9:30 p.m., I ask my dog Buffy, "Are you HUNGRY? Want your FOOD?"

I get her bowl from the same cupboard. I set it on the same counter. She jumps onto the same love seat and lies hanging over the edge, watching my every move. When her supper is ready, I place her bowl on the floor in the same spot I placed it last night. "Here's your FOOD! Time to EAT!"

While she eats, I clean up our own supper dishes.

When she finishes eating, I ask, "All DONE?" I put her bowl in the dishwasher and she waits confidently for the question she knows comes next. "Do you need to go OUT? Time to go OUT!"

> Exaggerate the key words. Pronounce them more deliberately than the other "filler" words in the sentence. Keep your sentences short and crisp. That's how you turn sounds into words for your dog.

Feed more than one meal a day

WHAT to feed your dog is a complicated question that I answer in another book I've written, called *Dog Care Wisdom: 11 Things You Must Do Right To Keep Your Dog Healthy and Happy.* It's available from my web site at *www.yourpurebredpuppy.com.*

If you're currently feeding your dog any brand of kibble or canned food, *Dog Care Wisdom* is a must-have book!

HOW OFTEN to feed your dog is a simpler question. Puppies, pregnant females, females nursing puppies, and dogs with certain health problems should eat three or four meals a day. All other dogs should eat twice a day.

No dog should eat only once a day, or else his stomach will growl, he will feel empty and uncomfortable, and he may even spit up white froth or bile. Think of how empty YOU feel when you haven't eaten all day.

Avoiding food guarding

It might seem natural to place your dog's food bowl in a distant corner or in his crate and leave him completely alone to eat it "in peace"…but it may lead to a dog who doesn't react properly if you ever need to interrupt his meal, or if a child accidentally intrudes upon his meal.

Assuming that your dog does not already have a food guarding problem, you can avoid one from ever developing by accustoming him to having people around while he is eating.

To avoid food guarding, follow these guidelines:

- Put your dog's bowl in the middle of the kitchen floor while you're cooking your own meal, or washing the dishes, or cleaning the countertop.
- At some point while your dog is eating, walk over to him and add a yummy treat (a piece of chicken or cheese, etc.) to his bowl. Say cheerfully, "Good FOOD" as you do so.
- At another point while he is eating (not necessarily the same meal), ask him, "Want some FOOD?" and pick up the bowl completely. Place a yummy treat into the bowl and return it to your dog: "Here's some FOOD!"

These simple techniques turn your presence and the removal of his food dish into good things in your dog's eyes.

If your dog is already showing signs of food guarding

First of all, how can you tell?

Well, if you approach your dog while he's eating and he...

- stops eating and stares at you
- or pushes his head deep into the bowl and freezes his body protectively
- or curls his lip or actually growls

...you have a problem.

What should you do?
Well, some common sense and
judgment is required here.

If your dog is a puppy and seems to be simply "acting out" with fussy growls and baby teeth, you should be able to use the respect training program in this book to change the pecking order in your household.

But if your dog is an adult and especially if he is large and/or truly aggressive (if he has ever snapped at or bitten anyone), you should call a local trainer who can evaluate him up close and personally.

If you believe it's safe and you want to try working with your dog on your own, here's what you might try

Prepare your dog's meal but don't put it in his regular bowl. Instead, put it in a separate dish, then place his regular food bowl (empty) on the floor.

He will run to the bowl and be surprised to find it empty. When he looks up at you inquiringly, bend down, holding the full dish of prepared food in your hand. Place two spoonfuls of the food into his empty bowl on the floor.

He will eat it quickly and look up for more. Repeat until the food is gone.

From your dog's point of view, having you near his food bowl is now a good thing! He had been guarding the bowl so you couldn't take food away—but now he sees that you're GIVING him food.

Do this for a full week. Then start him off with half a bowl of food, and when he finishes that, add the remaining half.

Then begin putting in the remaining half just before he finishes the first half—so you're actually adding food while he's eating. Soon you should be able to pick up the bowl while there's still food in it, so you can add the last half.

You might be wondering if you should simply correct your dog with a "No!" and a physical back-up, like you do for most undesirable behaviors. I don't recommend this for food guarding. Dogs who guard their food are often anxious and defensive, and if you give the wrong correction or a wrongly-timed correction, you could make things worse or end up bitten.

> It goes without saying that allowing a child around a dog who is guarding his food would be the height of idiocy.

Teach your dog to ask for water

Word #24: "Want Water?"

When your dog's water bowl is empty, lead him cheerfully over to the empty bowl and tap the bowl so he leans down to sniff it. Ask him, "Want WATER? WATER?" Try to keep his attention as you get the bottled water and pour it into his bowl. "Want WATER? Good WATER!"

When you give a name to this innocuous substance that your dog drinks, it takes on more importance in his eyes. Enough so that he may paw at his water bowl when it's empty, thereby letting you know it needs to be filled. He may even pick up the bowl and flip it around, or bring it to you. You can almost hear him saying, "WATER! There's supposed to be WATER in here!"

A variety of food words

Word #25: "Biscuit" (or "Treat")
Word #26: "Cookie" (or other food word)

Some owners call every treat a **treat** (or **biscuit**). Other owners prefer different words for different types of treats. Biscuit might be used for a commercial dog biscuit, while **cookie** or **cracker** or **cheese** might be used for these specific snacks.

Whichever words you decide to use, I like to establish a scheduled **Biscuit Time**—for example, mid-morning. Dogs love patterns and quickly learn to look forward to Biscuit Time. In this expectant frame of mind, they are ready and willing to listen to their new word and associate it with its tasty object.

There is one **disadvantage** to a fixed Biscuit Time: some dogs become too rigid about it. They start getting restless, pacing or whining or nudging you. They may even become upset if you're late.

With such rigid dogs, adhering to a schedule is not a good idea. Instead, offer their biscuit at random times—one day, give it in the morning, next day in the afternoon, third day in the evening. Occasionally skip the biscuit altogether. A random schedule makes rigid dogs less expectant and thus less stressed when things don't happen according to their expectations.

What should you do at Biscuit Time?

Ask your dog, "Want a BISCUIT? Who wants a BISCUIT? How about a BISCUIT?"

Proceed jauntily to the cupboard and take down the biscuit box. Rattle it and repeat with excitement, "Want a BISCUIT?"

Make a big show of taking the biscuit out of the box. Your dog may already be excited, but if this is your first time doing this, he may not know what it is. You may need to hold it near his nose to give him the idea.

It should be noted that some dogs couldn't care a fig about commercial dog biscuits. To get them excited, try a cheese cracker or oatmeal cookie. Never offer raisins or grapes—these can be toxic to dogs.

"Easy!" Teach your dog to be gentle

Once your dog is focused on the biscuit, he's going to lose interest fast if he doesn't get to eat it. But we want him to eat it in a **civilized** manner.

So we're going to add a polite behavior to Biscuit Time—your dog must take the treat GENTLY from your hand. He mustn't grab at it like a starving savage.

Word #27: "Easy!"

1. With your dog in front of you—it doesn't matter whether he's sitting or standing or even walking around—hold the treat in front of his mouth.

    Don't hold it too high or he'll jump for it, which is not the calm behavior you're trying to teach!

2. Say, "EEEE-zee." Draw it out as a long cautionary word, since you're cautioning him to be careful.

    If he tries to snatch at the treat, say, "Ah-Ah!" and jerk it away—don't let him have it. Caution him again, "EEEE-zee" and give him another chance to be a lady or a gentleman.

3. Only release the treat when he takes it gently from your fingers. And praise him quietly as he eats it: "GOOD boy. GOOD. GOOD BISCUIT."

> Your dog is being introduced to the idea that treats do not fall from the sky like manna from heaven, but rather are **earned** through positive behavior.

"Easy" is a word you'll use in many other circumstances, too. It's a **control word** that cautions your dog to be calm and gentle, so you can use it whenever he gets too excitable or engages in rough play.

Chapter 12

Basic Commands

Sit on command

In Chapter 10, you introduced "Sit" as a basic handling and grooming position by **placing** your dog into a sitting position with your hands. Now you're going to teach him to sit when you **tell** him to.

Your dog will learn to "Sit" before he gets his biscuit.

Think of it as his way of saying please.

- Your dog gives you something (a polite sit).
- Your dog gets something in return (a biscuit).

Here's how to teach it

1. With your dog standing (or dancing around!) in front of you, hold the biscuit so that it gets his attention.
2. When he's looking at the biscuit, say "Sit." Say it only once. Say it crisply. Pronounce that "t" at the end: "siTT." Your voice shouldn't go UP at the end—in other words, don't say "Sit?" as though you're begging him.
3. Move the treat away from your body and up to a level just above your dog's head. Because he has to bend his neck back to see the biscuit when it moves over his head, and because his neck

can't bend very far while he's in a standing position, he may automatically drop his hindquarters into a sitting position.

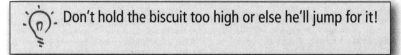 Don't hold the biscuit too high or else he'll jump for it!

If the movement of the biscuit doesn't encourage him to drop into a sit on his own, use your hands to place him into a sit. You already know how to do this from your grooming practice, but let's review:

One method is **Pull Up and Push Down**. With your right hand, pull up on his collar. With your left palm, push down on his hindquarters (just behind his two hipbones, or at the base of his tail). Be sure you're not pushing on his back—his spine and vertebrae are too sensitive for heavy pressure.

Another method is **The Fold**. Place your right palm on his chest. Place your left hand (if he's small) or your left forearm (if he's larger) across his rump (below his tail and above his knees). In one smooth motion, push his chest toward his rump, while tucking his back knees forward to **fold** him into a sit over your hand or forearm.

4. However you accomplish it, the moment your dog is sitting, tell him "GOOD sit." This is one time when you should keep your praise quiet and calm. If you praise too enthusiastically, he will get excited and start jumping around.

5. Take your hands off him.

    If he holds his sit for even a couple of seconds, give him the treat.

    If he doesn't hold the sit, don't give him the treat. Use your hands to replace him in the sitting position. If he gets up again, reposition him again, but be firmer. If he continues to stand up, use one hand to hold him in position. In the beginning, you want him to succeed, even if he needs help. After a couple of seconds holding him in position, give him the treat.

6. When you give him the treat, raise your voice into a cheerful "Okay!" This is the same **release word** (Word #12) you used to let him out of his crate. "Okay!" means that he no longer needs to hold his sitting position. At first you may have to encourage him to move, but he'll quickly learn what "Okay" means. In fact, it will become one of his favorite words!

7. Pick up a second biscuit and repeat the exercise. Then repeat one more time, for a total of three times. And that's enough for one session.

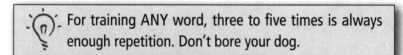 For training ANY word, three to five times is always enough repetition. Don't bore your dog.

Within a few days, your dog should catch on and begin sitting when you say "Sit"—or at the very least, he should begin holding the sit once you guide him into it with your hands.

If after a few days he's still not doing it, you'll need to become more insistent. Use a sharper tug on his collar and a firmer push on his hindquarters. You want to send the message that he would be much more comfortable if he sat himself rather than waiting for your "guidance"!

If he is sitting properly on command, but keeps breaking the sitting position before you tell him "Okay", start saying, "Ah-ah" **AS he breaks position.**

Timing is very important here—he must hear the "Ah-ah" AS he is getting up, so that he'll associate the corrective word with the action of **breaking** the sit.

Also, when you replace him in the sitting position after he has broken it, be firmer with your hands and voice. Again, the message should be that you're not going to keep helping him forever—that he needs to start doing it right or face a correction.

In other words, you're switching from gentle guidance to firmer correction.

Lie down

Word #28: "Lie Down" (Or "Down")

 "Down" means your dog should lie down. Try to use "Down" only for that specific purpose—to tell your dog to assume a lying down position.

I don't recommend using "Down" to mean "Get off the furniture" or "Stop jumping on people." "Off" is a better word in those cases. (We'll learn "Off" later in this chapter.) For jumping on people, you can also simply use "No" or "Stop that" reinforced with a physical back-up, just as with any other unacceptable behavior.

There are three ways to teach your dog to lie down.

Hands only (the gentlest method)

1. Put on your dog's leash and have him sit on your left side. Crouch or kneel beside him, on his right side. Tuck the leash under your knees so both your hands are free.
2. Place your left hand, **palm down**, on top of his shoulders. You can hook your fingers in his collar, if you like, for more control.
3. Place your right hand and wrist, **palm up**, against the BACK of his front legs, down around the level of his ankles.
4. Say, "Down" and sweep your right hand and arm forward and slightly upward. This scoops his front legs forward and slightly upward so his legs come to rest across your hand and wrist—and maybe across your forearm, too, if he's a big dog.

5. At the same time you're sweeping his front legs forward and slightly upward with your right hand, push down on his shoulders with your **left** hand—and with both hands working together, lower him into a lying down position. Repeat "Down" as he goes down.

Hands and leash

If your dog is too antsy when you fiddle with his front legs, rest your left hand on his shoulders as before, but instead of placing your right hand behind his legs, grasp the leash very close to his collar—just below the snap.

Say, "Down" and push down on his shoulders at the same time as you pull or tug the leash downward **and slightly to the right.** (Pulling straight down makes it too easy for your dog to brace himself and resist, while pulling slightly to the right throws him off-balance a bit and encourages him to sink into a lying down position.) Repeat "Down" as he goes down.

Foot and leash

I recommend this method only for dogs who strenuously resist (or growl) when being physically handled.

1. Put on your dog's leash and have him sit.
2. Hold the end of the leash in your right hand so it forms a large U-shaped loop between your hand and your dog's collar.
3. Say, "Down" and step on the U-shaped loop with your left foot as you pull the leash upward with your right hand. You're using your foot as a pulley, you see.

    As you pull the leash up on YOUR side of the foot pulley, your dog's head should be pulled smoothly down to the floor on HIS side of the foot pulley. Repeat "Down" as he goes down.

Now, the Foot-and-Leash method doesn't always go smoothly, which is why I recommend it only as a last resort. Often a dog will struggle as his head is pulled toward the floor by unseen forces. If you keep up the pressure calmly, many dogs will eventually relax and lie down, but some dogs will continue to resist.

Make sure you're planting your foot pulley properly. Your foot pressure should be firm enough so the leash doesn't slip out, yet with enough "wiggle space" underneath the sole of your shoe so the leash can slide as you pull it upward. You may need to experiment with different shoes to find one that allows the leash to slide properly.

Make sure the loop is formed fairly close to your dog's collar. If the loop is too far away, there will be a lot of leash to slide through your foot pulley and your dog will have more time to brace against it and struggle. Experiment with forming the loop at different places along the leash until you find the most effective fulcrum point.

Lie down for 30 minutes

Now. Once your dog is lying down, you're only halfway there. Now you need to KEEP him lying down—for 30 minutes.

Yes, 30 minutes!

In most obedience classes, your dog learns to lie down and stay for three minutes while you stand at the end of the leash. Unfortunately, in real life, this is useless!

Say you have guests over. After your dog greets people, you want him to lie down. You don't want to have to stand at the end of his leash and stare at him—and three minutes is much too short a time to be helpful.

No, what you want is a dog who will lie down in a corner of the room, off leash, while everyone else moves freely around the room. After awhile, you can allow him up to stretch, visit, go outside, etc. A reasonable time for him to remain down is a half hour or so.

You might think your dog will never stay down for 30 minutes, but he will. In fact, it's EASIER for him to stay lying down for **thirty** minutes than for **three** minutes!

Why? Because during a 3-minute down, he is waiting the whole time to get up. He watches you intently, shifts restlessly, tenses his muscles whenever you look in his direction. He is poised for the slightest sign that the three minutes are up.

Whereas, during a 30-minute down, most dogs relax and go to sleep.

How to teach the 30-minute "Long Down"

After you place your dog down, hold him there for a few seconds with your hands, praising him softly. Then remove your hands. He will probably jump right up.

The **INSTANT** he starts to get up—don't wait until he's all the way up!—use your hands and/or the leash to stop him, and patiently place him back down.

It is essential that you be **quick** here! Don't give your dog time to jump all the way up and cavort around. As soon as he begins to rise, dart your hands in there and replace him in the down position—or tug him back down with the leash—or both.

Patience and persistence are the keys to this very important exercise in control. The first time you try this exercise, your dog may get up 100 times. No problem! You will replace him 100 times.

**This is an exercise, pure and simple, of
who can outlast the other.**

If YOU don't give up, your dog will eventually sigh and stay down—and as far as leadership goes, you will have just taken a giant step forward in his eyes!

> There's an old saying: The stonecutter hammers at his rock a hundred times without so much as a crack showing. Yet at the hundred and first blow it splits in two, and it was not that blow that did it—but all that had gone before. —*Jacob Riis*

Amusing antics your dog might try during the Long Down

He might stare at you

- It might be an intent stare as he tries to send you a telepathic message: "I want to get up right now."
- It might be an eager-beaver stare: "Time to get up now? Huh? Is it?"
- It might be a hopeful stare: "Wouldn't you rather play with me? Can I crawl into your lap?"
- It might be a pitiful stare: "This is awful. You're so mean to me. I feel miserable."

> Or he might flatten his ears and refuse to look at you at all, his body language clearly saying, "Fine, then. Have it your way. I'm never talking to you again."

Your response to all of these should be

Ignore it. Don't make eye contact with him. Many dogs interpret eye contact as an invitation to interact with you. In fact, your dog may try very hard to make eye contact during the Long Down so he can assume his most charming or pathetic expression and persuade you to stop this foolish exercise and play with him instead.

He might inch forward

"There, that didn't hurt anything, did it? After all, I'm still lying down. How about another inch? How about two inches? Gosh, I'm a little stiff…how about a big s-t-r-e-t-c-h of my front legs…ohh, that felt good…let's try another stretch…let's crawl a little while we're at it…"

Your response should be

Don't allow the first inch. Scoot him immediately back to his original position. With a small- to medium-sized dog, you can often slide him back without even raising him from the down position.

Be careful with your hands here. Don't stroke or pet your dog as you slide him. Believe it or not, some dogs will deliberately crawl around just so you'll put your hands on their body when you move them back. Be quick and businesslike as you slide your dog back to his original position and immediately get your hands off him.

He might discover imaginary fleas

"They're so itchy! I MUST sit up and scratch them!"

Your response should be

There are no fleas. Place him back down without waiting for him to finish scratching. If you wait, as soon as he's done he will stand up and amble away, hoping you've forgotten about this whole stupid exercise.

He might nibble at the carpet, or chew on his leash, or whine or bark at you

"I need something to do! I'm so bored!"

Your response should be

Tug the leash. "No. Stop that."

He might shift position by rolling from one hip to the other, or flop onto his side so he's sprawled flat

Your response should be

Nothing. Your dog doesn't have to be a statue. He just has to stay lying down in his original **place**.

Just watch out for the clever dog who tries to extend his flop into a Roll Over trick, which puts him well away from his original position. If he rolls all the way over, put him back in his original position so he's not tempted to go any further.

Three reasons why the Long Down is one of the most valuable exercises you can teach your dog

1. The Long Down is practical. Every owner, at one point or another, needs his or her dog to lie down and stay put.
2. The Long Down is calming. Your dog learns to relax and be patient—qualities that are especially important to instill in energetic or excitable dogs.
3. The Long Down establishes you as a leader. Your dog learns that sometimes he has to do something simply because you say so. Yes, it's boring. He isn't being petted or cuddled or spoken

to. He can't entertain himself by chewing on a toy. He has to just lie there quietly—because YOU want him to.

 There is no better exercise than this one for establishing leadership with your dog!

Releasing your dog from the Long Down

When the half hour is up, call out in a cheerful voice, "Okay, Jake!" and encourage him to get up. It won't take much encouragement!

It is very important that YOU always be the one to release your dog from the Long Down. If anything interrupts you before the half hour is up (say, the phone or the doorbell), release your dog with "Okay!" and get him up before you walk away.

Otherwise he will almost certainly get up while you're busy elsewhere, and you won't be able to correct him from a distance. So think ahead and release him first.

 Don't ever let him think he can decide for himself when to get up.

Practice the Long Down every day. As your dog gets more reliable, you can progress to sitting in a chair and watching TV or reading a book. Just keep one eye on him. You don't want him wandering around the room while you're engrossed in Chapter Six!

When you can depend on your dog to stay put while you're right there beside him, begin standing up and walking around the room. Eventually you should be able to leave the room for a minute or two and return to find him still lying down where you left him.

What a marvelous exercise in self-control!

Growling or snapping when you work on "Down"

Growling or snapping is a frightening sign of disrespect. A growling dog believes that he is higher in the pecking order than you are, and that you have no right to be handling him or making him do anything he doesn't want to do.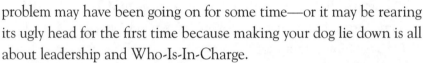

This is an attitude problem, a relationship problem between you and your dog. The problem may have been going on for some time—or it may be rearing its ugly head for the first time because making your dog lie down is all about leadership and Who-Is-In-Charge.

Dominant dogs instinctively recognize that if they give in on this exercise, they are allowing you to be the leader—and some of them are not willing to do that without a fight.

> **Caution!** Some common sense and judgment are
> required here.

If your dog is a puppy and is simply "acting out" with fussy growls and baby teeth, you should be able to use the respect training program presented in this book to change the pecking order in your household and bring him under your control.

But if your dog is an adult and especially if he is large and/or truly aggressive, you should call a local trainer for an up-close evaluation and assistance.

Speaking for myself personally, I would not keep a dog who wouldn't "let" me place him into a Down position. What else might he decide I can't do? I would never trust him and I would never feel confident of my ability to handle him in an emergency.

If you do want to try working with an aggressive dog on your own, here's what you might try

Adapt the Long Down exercise as follows:

With your dog on leash, sit on a chair. Tuck most of the leash under your behind so you're sitting on it. Measure out just enough leash so your dog could lie down (if he wanted to) right beside the chair. Give him no more leash than that.

But he doesn't HAVE to lie down. He is free to sit or stand, if he wants to. So this isn't really a Long Down exercise, but it IS an exercise in control and leadership...

...because you are going to limit his actions. If he stands on his hind legs and puts his paws on you, snap the leash downward. If he barks at you or nudges at you, snap the leash sideways. If he chews on the leash, snap it out of his mouth. Add "No" or "Stop that" to each snap.

Since you are correcting him when he jumps, barks, nudges, paws, or chews, and since the very short leash doesn't allow him to go anywhere, and since you will not pet him or talk to him or even look at him, he will eventually decide to just stand or sit or lie down quietly. Good! Round One goes to you!

Here's what else you should do with a growling dog

Neuter him. Testosterone makes dominance problems much worse. Neutering will lower your dog's hormonal levels so that he doesn't feel so compelled to be in charge.

Don't breed any dog who has growled at you. Such genes should never be passed on.

Confine him. A growling dog should not be allowed freedom of the house. Put his leash on him and attach the other end to your waist. Now he must follow you around. Both physically and psychologically, this helps establish you as the leader and him as the follower.

Work hard on this 100 Words program. It will increase your dog's respect for you. After you've taught him all the obedience words, practice a quick succession of them, for five minutes straight, several times a day. "Heel. Sit. Stay. Come. Sit. Down." Again, this is the leader-follower dynamic where you are giving commands and he is following them. Good for building respect!

Finally, for a growling dog, I recommend a book called *People, Pooches, and Problems,* by Job Michael Evans. Job passed away some years ago and is sorely missed by the dog training community. He loved dogs dearly but he brooked no nonsense from them when they acted up. His *Radical Regimen for Recalcitrant Rovers* program is must-reading for anyone with an aggressive dog. It meshes well with the Respect Training Program you're learning now.

Teach your dog his name

Word #29: Your Dog's Name

1.   Put a handful of treats in your pocket, and with your dog on leash, wander around your house or yard. When his attention is elsewhere, say, when he is sniffing something, stop walking and say his name clearly, "Jake!"
2.   If he doesn't immediately look at you, give a gentle tug on the leash. Not a correction—just a very gentle tug to get his attention. The instant he looks at you, praise him, "Good boy!" and give him a treat.
3.   Resume walking. When his attention has wandered away from you again, repeat the exercise. After three to five repetitions—no more!—stop for that session.

It shouldn't be long before your dog looks at you immediately when you say his name.

> -ʘ- Remember this guideline of three to five repetitions.
> Whether you're teaching your dog something new or
> practicing something he already knows, do it only three to five
> times. More than that is boring.

Watch me (Pay attention)

Now we're going to teach your dog to sit still and pay attention to you.

Word #30: "Watch Me"

STEP ONE

1. Put your dog's leash on and lead him into a quiet room.
2. Tell him to "Sit" and stand in front of him, facing him. With a small dog, kneel in front of him.
3. Put one hand under your dog's chin and your other hand on his forehead. Tilt his head up so he is looking into your eyes.
4. Say, "Jake. WATCH me. WATCH me."
5. Look into his eyes for fifteen seconds, gently stroking him under the chin and repeating quietly, "Jake. Watch me. Watch me. Good."
6. After fifteen seconds, remove your hands and say quietly, "Good boy." Unsnap the leash and let him go.

> -ʘ- Practice this enforced eye contact twice a day for a full
> week. It seems like a simple little exercise, I know—but
> it shows your dog that you can restrain his movements and keep
> him calm and focused. This is a powerful lesson in leadership!

STEP TWO

For the second week, put your dog's leash on and have him sit beside you on your left side. He should be facing the same direction you are, his head and ears about six inches from your left leg. This position is called **Heel Position**.

The goal here is simple. He must remain sitting beside you. If he stands up or lies down or walks away, use your hands and/or the leash to replace him in the same sitting position beside you.

If he continues to break position, start saying, "Ah-ah!" AS he breaks position and replace him more firmly—with a sharper tug on his collar and a sterner push on his hindquarters.

When he will remain sitting for ten seconds, the next step is for him to **pay attention** to you.

Have him sit in Heel Position, then say his name, "Jake." He should look up at you—but he must not get up! Put him back in position if he does.

Once he is looking at you AND holding his sit position, say in a calm voice, "Watch me." If he keeps looking at you for even a second or two, praise him. "Good watch."

Then raise your voice into a cheerful "Okay!"—the release word. You may have to encourage him to move by walking forward yourself and guiding him with the leash so he breaks out of the Sit position and begins moving around. But he'll quickly learn what "Okay" means.

Over the next few weeks, increase the time you ask your dog to look at you. Start with just a couple of seconds and build up to ten seconds. During these longer times, occasionally remind him, "WATCH me. Good. Watch me."

Now. That's how the exercise is supposed to go! But what if it doesn't go so smoothly?

If your dog doesn't respond to his name at all

You need to go back to teaching your dog his name, Word #29. You'll be walking around your house and yard with your dog on leash, occasionally saying his name, rewarding with a treat when he looks at you, reminding him with a gentle tug on the leash when he doesn't.

If your dog keeps getting distracted and looking away

There are several things you can try.

Move your index finger near his eyes to catch his attention. Then draw your finger quickly back toward your own eyes to remind him where you want him to focus. Do this rapidly in a flicking motion.

With a large dog whose head is close to your left hand, tap his skull gently with your fingers. Trainer Diane Bauman calls this, "Knock, knock! Anybody home?" Or use your left hand to gently(!) tug on his cheek or beard.

Tug on the leash to get and keep his attention.

Hold a treat or toy near your mouth so he must look up at you to see it. Move it around slightly as you remind him, "Watch me." At the end of the exercise, after you release him, give him the treat or toy.

This one often works like magic—but don't fool yourself. Your dog is really looking at the treat or toy, not at you. The whole point of this exercise is for your dog to pay attention to YOU. So if you resort to this trick, do it only for a short time.

If nothing else works, lift his head with your hands and hold it so that he must look at you.

> "Watch me" is an important concept for your dog to learn. If he won't pay attention to you, it will be harder to teach other words that require his attention.

Come when called

Word #31: "Come"

Along with "No," "Come" is the most important word in your dog's vocabulary. For the rest of his life, your dog should never hear the word "Come" without being required to obey it.

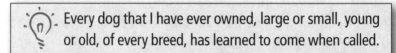 Every dog that I have ever owned, large or small, young or old, of every breed, has learned to come when called.

Unlike fun words such as "Shake hands" or "Roll over," where it doesn't really matter whether your dog learns it or not, "Come" is a mandatory word that must be mastered.

Three steps in teaching "Come"

Study each step carefully before you start working with your dog. Don't skip any of the steps! The first two steps are on leash so you can MAKE your dog come if he chooses not to.

Because remember:

For the rest of his life, your dog should never hear the word "Come" without being required to obey it. In the beginning, you need a leash to guarantee that your dog comes every single time he hears the word.

Step #1 in teaching "Come"

1. Put a handful of treats in your pocket, and with your dog on leash, wander around your house or yard. When his attention is elsewhere, say, when he is sniffing something, stop walking and say his name clearly, "Jake!"

This sounds familiar, doesn't it? You did this when you were teaching your dog his name. When he hears his name, he should turn to look at you.

2.   When your dog looks at you in response to his name, crouch down, open your arms invitingly, and call in a happy voice, "Come!"

3.   The instant he starts toward you, pat your hands together gently—don't startle or scare him—as you praise and encourage him, "Come—good boy!"

Make sure the leash hangs completely loose as he comes toward you—don't reel him in like a fish!

4.   As he approaches you, don't reach out to grab him. Keep encouraging him with your hands and voice to come all the way to you until his nose or head touches (or practically touches) you.

5.   Pet and praise him for a few moments, then tell him, Okay!" to let him know he doesn't need to stay near you any longer.

6.   Begin walking again, and when he wanders to the end of the leash and becomes distracted again, repeat the exercise.

 But what if...?

What if he doesn't come to you?
What if he comes partway, but stops?
What if he comes to you, but runs past you?
Ah, that's why you attached the leash! Use it to guide him to you, then praise him as though he had come on his own. You want him to succeed every time at doing the action that fits the word.

One way or another, he must come to you.

Practice indoors. Practice outdoors in your yard. In both locations, keep the leash on so he MUST come.

Give him dozens of experiences hearing the word "Come!" and dozens of experiences coming toward you.

Praise and encourage him the instant he starts moving toward you, as well as when he arrives. Occasionally give him a treat.

Step #2 in teaching "Come"

After a week of practice in your house and yard, we're ready to practice away from home. Take your dog for a walk. When he is distracted by something, such as sniffing a fire hydrant or watching another dog across the street...

1. Stop walking. Stand still. (It's okay if HE keeps walking.)
2. Call, "Jake, come!" and immediately start backing up—TROT backward.
3. If your dog responded properly to your Come command, he will already be moving toward you. As you back up, make sure the leash hangs completely loose—don't reel him in. Pat your hands together and encourage him, "Come, good boy, come!"
4. After backing up about ten feet, stop walking, but keep encouraging your dog to come all the way to you. Praise and pet him, then tell him, Okay!" and continue your walk. Watch for another distraction so you can call him again.

But what if he doesn't come?

That's why a leash is so essential!

If your dog ignored your Come command and just stands there, it will be only a moment before you reach the end of the leash. You're backing up, remember?

When you reach the end of the leash, keep going! If your dog is inattentive or focused on something other than you, he's going to get a pretty strong jerk that will compel him to come toward you—and once he does start moving toward you, pat your hands together and encourage him. Keep backing up, making him cover a goodly amount of ground. Then stop and act as though he had come to you on his own—praise him with enthusiasm!

 The message should be that **Coming To You** is always associated with goodness.

Step #3 (final step!) in teaching "Come"

With your dog's leash attached, take him outside in your yard and drop your end of the leash. Watch for a time when he's wandering around, not looking at you. Call cheerfully, "Jake, come!" If he comes all the way to you, praise!

If he doesn't come—if he ignores you, or just stands there looking at you, or heads off in another direction—repeat, "Jake, COME!" once more, in a firm, serious voice. If he responds to your stronger tone and comes all the way to you, praise him happily.

But if he still doesn't come, don't say another word.

JUST GO GET HIM.

As you walk toward your disobedient dog, he may move away from you. No problem—you remember from Chapter 1 what you should do if your dog runs away from you, don't you?

That's right.

- Track him down silently.
- Don't say anything.
- Don't run.

Walk firmly and purposefully, keeping your expression stony-faced, drilling your dog with your eyes.

Baffled and unnerved by your persistent, methodical following, your dog will most likely, fairly quickly, shrink down and give up. Or you will get close enough to step on the end of the leash and stop him in his tracks.

So. Whether he just stood there waiting for you, or whether you had to track him down, the goal is to get hold of his leash.

Once you have the leash in your hand, give it a good snap (just a tug for very small or sensitive dogs—use common sense!) to propel him in your direction. Then start trotting backward, saying, "Come! Come! Come!" Your voice should be quite firm here—not cheerful. After all these weeks, your dog knows darned well what "Come!" means, yet he chose to ignore it.

Back up all the way to the point at which you were standing when you first called him—the point at which, had he obeyed this word that he fully knows, he would have ended up. When you both arrive there, change your attitude dramatically. Smile! Praise him! Pet him! Scoop him up, if he's small! Do whatever gets his tail wagging!

The message you want to send is this:

"The place where I am when I call you (Point A) is a happy place full of praise and petting. If you come to me on your own, you'll get all that praise and petting immediately.

If you don't come on your own, I'll come get you and it will not be a happy experience. I'll correct you all the way from Point B (wherever you are when I catch you) to Point A (where I gave the command in the first place). So you see that you end up in the same place anyway. Now, wouldn't you rather do that the easy way?"

> This is a critical lesson for your dog to learn—namely, that one way or the other he has to do what you say, and that doing it right away, on his own, is much more comfortable and rewarding than being made to do it.

Practice this exercise every day until your dog is rock-solid. Then replace the dragging leash with a shorter hand-hold (we talked about hand-holds in Chapter 1). A hand-hold gives you something to grab if you need to catch and correct him.

> **To sum up, then:**
> For the rest of your dog's life, each and every time you say "Come!" you must see to it that he does so. One way or another, he must end up at the point where you called him.

With this word more than any other...

if you are not in a position to enforce it—should he happen to choose this particular instance to disobey it—for example, if you're on the phone, or in the shower, or on a ladder painting the house, and you know that you won't be able to go get him quickly if he disobeys you...don't call him.

Wait (stay inside open doors and gates)

Word #32: "Wait"

Be honest—has anything like this ever happened at your house?

"Watch out for the dog!" Kathy cried. Her friend Mary Sue had just arrived and started to pull open the screen door so she could come into the kitchen.

Spotting the crack of daylight, Jake made a mad dash for it. Mary Sue leaped backward and managed to slam the screen door a millisecond before Jake barreled into it, leaving yet another nose print in the battered black mesh.

Mary Sue looked down through the screen at the Armstrong's exuberant dog. "What a nuisance," she thought.

This behavior is unacceptable for two reasons:

First, it could cost your dog his life. If he gets through the door and spies some temptation running down the street—a cat or a squirrel, say—he will probably take off and end up hit by a car. It happens all the time.

Second, it's unfair to your guests. Visitors shouldn't have to be paranoid about your dog barreling past them. As our dogs' guardians, we have the responsibility of teaching them to stay put, even when a door or gate tempts them.

So here's a better story. Mary Sue had just arrived at Kathy's house and started to pull open the screen door.

Jake bounded toward the opening, but Kathy called, "Jake, wait!" and Mary Sue watched as the exuberant dog skidded to a stop and stood still, wriggling eagerly, waiting for her to come all the way in.

Mary Sue stepped inside, closed the door behind her, and looked down at Jake. "He's so well-behaved!" she thought.

Yes, a much better story!

Here's how to teach "Wait"

1. You and your dog are inside your house. With his leash attached, walk toward the front door as though the two of you are heading out for a walk.

    If you have a screen door on the outside of your front door, prop it open ahead of time so it won't be in the way when you open the front door. In other words, when that front door opens, you want your dog to see an "open shot" to the Great Outdoors.

2. When you reach the front door, tighten the leash, say, "Jake, wait" and open the door.

3. Your dog will probably try to rush out. Say "Ah-ah" and use **alternating pressure** on the leash to show him that you don't want him to go through the door.

    Alternating pressure means you tighten the leash only enough to PULL him slightly backward, then you quickly loosen it to give him a choice again. Be quick! Don't let him get all the way through the door before you pull him back. Tighten the leash the instant his toes go over the threshold and loosen it the instant his toes are back inside.

    Your first few pulls should be just strong enough to slide/drag/propel him back into the house. But if he continues to rush for the door each time you loosen the leash, make your pulls sharper, more like a corrective jerk.

    Use common sense! TUG a Chihuahua! Gently!

4. You may need to "check" your dog with the leash a couple of times or you may need to do it ten (or more!) times. It doesn't matter. When the light bulb finally goes on and he WAITS inside the open door **with no tension** on the leash, praise him quietly. (Don't get him all excited.)

5. Close the door and lead him into another room for a short break, then head toward the front door again and repeat the exercise a second time, and then a third time.

 Three times is enough for one session. You can do another session of three "Waits" later in the day, if you wish.

"Wait" on a completely loose leash

After practicing "Wait" for a couple of days as described above, make one important change. As you approach the front door, don't tighten the leash at all. Keep it loose. Just say, "Wait" and open the door.

Without the reminder of the tight leash, your dog may try to rush through when the door opens. The instant his toe crosses the threshold, say "Ah-ah" and tug him firmly back inside the house. Once he's inside, say again, "Wait" and slacken the leash to give him another opportunity to rush through.

And another, and another, and another, until he accepts the reality that "Wait" means the same thing today as it meant yesterday—not to go through the door.

The choice is ultimately his—your job is simply to provide the consequences. Each time he steps out, he is tugged back in, which makes it crystal clear that stepping over the threshold gets him nothing but discomfort.

> Dog training means providing your dog with opportunities to take some action while you provide a positive or negative consequence to that action.

Your dog will do what benefits him most and he will avoid doing what makes him uncomfortable. It's up to you to provide the benefits (praise, petting, treats) and the discomforts (corrections) so he will make the choices you prefer or that are best/safest for him.

When your dog finally stays inside the house **with the leash loose** and the front door open, praise him quietly.

Close the door and lead him into another room for a short break, then head toward the front door again and repeat the whole exercise a second time, and then a third time.

"Wait" with distractions

The next step in practicing "Wait" is to add distractions. When the front door is open and your dog is standing there and the leash is loose:

- Hum or whistle a happy tune.
- Do a few knee bends or jumping jacks.
- Talk to an imaginary visitor at the door.
- Sit in a chair near the door (inside the house) and read aloud from a book.

What should your dog be doing during this time? Well, he can just stand there, or sit, or lie down, or walk around within the limits of the leash. It's his choice. He simply can't pass through the open door. (No barking, either!)

Is he still waiting? Good!

- Have your son walk by, OUTSIDE the door.
- Have your daughter walk by, bouncing a ball.
- Have your son run by.
- Have your daughter skip rope in the front yard.

Whether it's you or your kids providing a distraction, it must be done in a way that's fair to your dog. Don't speak to your dog. Don't look directly at him. No teasing!

When your dog is doing well with distractions on a regular leash, graduate to a 20-foot leash or rope. Now you can get quite a distance from him—always staying inside your house, of course. Your dog may choose to walk around the room with you, or he may decide to hang out near the open front door, peering out. The only thing he cannot do is cross the threshold (or bark or chew on the woodwork!)

"Wait" while YOU go outside

Switch back to a shorter leash. With the front door open and both of you standing there, repeat, "Wait." Now YOU step over the threshold. Keep some tension on the leash—upward and backward—as you step through, to help hold your dog in position on HIS side of the door.

As soon as your foot hits the ground outside, turn and face him. Now he should be inside the house, and you should be just barely outside, on the porch or stoop, holding tension on the leash to keep him indoors.

Caution him, "Wait" and loosen the leash. He may try to rush outside to join you. The instant his toe crosses the threshold, use the leash to bounce him back inside the house. You stay put on your side. Once he's back inside, caution him, "Wait" and loosen the leash again to give him another chance to either rush out or stay put.

No matter how many times you have to bounce him back inside, when he does finally stand there—actually, he can stand or sit or lie down or even walk back and forth, just so long as he stays on his side of the threshold—he has just done a marvelous "Wait."

Praise him. But softly, so he isn't tempted to rush out to you. "Good boy. Wait. Good boy." Hold up your hand like a stop sign, to help remind him.

Finally, say, "Okay! Come!" That should bring him running across the threshold! If not, use the leash to encourage him to join you outside. "Good boy!"

> Now it's simply a matter of getting further away from the door—gradually—and adding more tempting distractions as your dog waits inside.

Sometimes, instead of calling him outside to join you, go back inside the house, praise your dog for waiting, and close the door. In other words, don't always give him an "Okay!" to come out.

In practical life, as you know, there will be many times when you need to go outside for a moment by yourself—say, to accept a package from UPS. Then you'll go back inside the house without your dog ever being allowed out. So he should learn right upfront that he doesn't always get to cross the boundary after "Wait."

Other places to practice "Wait"

Have your dog "Wait" before going INTO your house, too. For example, after a walk, say, "Wait" and open the front door but don't let him go IN until you've given the "Okay."

Have him "Wait" at the back door before you let him out into the yard. Or have him "Wait" before coming into the house from the yard, after a potty trip.

Have him "Wait" before going through sliding patio doors.

Have him "Wait" before going in—or out—of the gate to your property.

Have him "Wait" on one side of an open doorway, such as the doorway between your kitchen and living room.

Have him "Wait" at the top of the stairs before going down. Or at the bottom of the stairs before going up.

> Don't ask your dog to "Wait" OFF-LEASH anywhere where he could dash into a busy street. A dog will always choose the worst possible moment to forget or ignore a word—and all it takes is once for your dog to be dead.

Teach your dog to "Wait" inside your car

When your dog is in the back seat of your car, you should be able to open the car door without him jumping out.

Word #33: "Go car"

With your dog on leash, walk toward your parked car. When you reach the rear door, say, "Wait" and open the door. The first couple of times, hold the leash slightly taut to remind him of what this word means.

When you do loosen the leash, be prepared to check your dog quickly if he tries to jump in. Once he is waiting at the open car door with the leash loose, tell him, "Okay! GO CAR!" and encourage him to jump in. Help him, if necessary, by using your hands to boost him up—or use treats to motivate him. Pick up a small dog and physically place him into the back seat.

Now for the hard part! Close the door and let him stay in the car alone for ten seconds. Then caution him (through the closed door) to "Wait." Open the door and quickly get hold of the leash so you can stop him if he tries to jump out. Caution him again, "Wait" and completely loosen the leash to give him the opportunity to stay in or jump out.

And another opportunity, and another, and another, until he realizes that "Wait" means the same inside the car as it did inside your house. "Good boy!" Close the door and repeat the exercise.

After three to five repetitions, let him come out. "Okay, Jake!" That should bring him bounding out. (If he is small, lift him out yourself—don't let him injure himself by jumping.)

When he's no longer making any attempt to jump out when the door opens, make the exercise more challenging. Switch to your 20-foot leash so you can get further away from the open car door, yet still have control over him if he should leap out.

Oh, and add distractions—you know about distractions!

Riding safely in the car

When we practiced "Wait," your dog was loose in the back seat while he was learning not to jump out of the car. But it isn't safe for him to RIDE loose in the back seat.

As Jake leaped—for the third time—from the back seat into the front seat, Roger startled and jerked the steering wheel violently to one side. "Jake!" he shouted. "For the love of Pete, will you settle down?"

With the wind whistling in through the open windows, Jake couldn't hear anything. The excited dog thrust his head out the passenger window, squinting his eyes against the wind. He bounded across the front seat and into Roger's lap, craning his neck out the driver's window to see if things were more interesting over there.

"Jake!" cried Roger, shoving at the dog and struggling to steer with one hand. Jake leaped into the back seat again, plunked his paws onto the rear window ledge, and began barking vigorously at a motorcycle behind them. "Jake!" Roger shouted in vain.

If you allow your dog to ride loose in the car

You're putting your dog, yourself, your passengers, and every other driver and passenger on the road in danger.

In a crash, warns a highway safety article in *Readers Digest,* loose objects, including pets, become deadly projectiles. In a 30 mph crash, a 15-pound object loose in the back seat continues hurtling forward at 30 mph until it strikes someone or something with 300 pounds of force.

In other words, even a Miniature Schnauzer, because of **momentum**, becomes the equivalent of two Saint Bernards hurtling forward to fracture the skull or break the neck of someone in the front seat.

> The Institute for Highway Safety says, "After the collision **outside,** there are always collisions **inside. Both wreak havoc."**

Your loose dog may not only cause injuries during an accident, he may actually cause the accident by jostling your arm or engaging in some antic that distracts you from paying full attention to the road.

And it's not just you and other people who will be hurt. Your loose dog will be battered against the windshield, or flung through an open or shattered window or door into the street. The impact will injure or kill him or set him loose in traffic, where he will take off in a panic and be lost or hit by another car.

Please, folks, if you truly care about your dog, **secure him in the rear seat:**

- with a special canine harness and seat belt like the Ruff Rider Safety Harness *(www.ruffrider.com).*
- or in a crate that has itself been buckled into the rear seat so IT can't hurtle around the car during a crash.

Don't buckle your dog into the **front** seat of a car with airbags. Airbags blast out of the dashboard at a fearsome speed that can kill a dog.

Too idiotic for words

- Riding on your lap while you drive?
- Riding in the open bed of a pickup truck?
- Riding on the rear window shelf?

Along with using "Go car!" for actually getting into the car, you can also use it to cue your dog that a ride in the car is imminent.

> Attaching a word to an upcoming event helps your dog develop the mental skill of visualizing that event and anticipating the fun that goes with it.

While you're still in the house, ask him, "Go car?" Then follow up immediately by clipping on his leash and heading toward the car.

Make sure there's no delay! Don't ask your dog if he wants to go for a ride, then get bogged down looking for his leash, checking the weather, finding the right jacket, visiting the bathroom, grabbing a snack, or answering the phone.

Make your preparations ahead of time. Find out what the weather is and decide which jacket you're going to wear. Put a snack in your pocket. Go to the bathroom. Check to see that his leash is in the closet where you thought it was.

THEN ask your dog, "Go car?" and whisk him out to the car right away.

"What if my dog doesn't like riding in the car?"

Well, has he had the chance to associate car rides with a fun time? Or does he only ride to the vet's office or to the groomer or boarding kennel? If so, he is likely to have an unpleasant association with car rides and your cheerful "Go for a ride in the car?" may send him running into his crate or under the bed.

You may be able to fix this by taking your dog to fun places. Drive him to the park. To the woods. To the beach. Even if only a block away! Play cheerful music and sing along. Have someone ride along with you and feed your dog his favorite treats.

The goal is to give your dog pleasant associations with the car so he will change his opinion of it.

Sit-Stay

When you were teaching your dog to pay attention to you (Word #30: "Watch me!"), you taught him to sit quietly beside you. But what if you want him to stay sitting even when you're not standing beside him?

Word #34: "Stay"

1. Start with your dog sitting in Heel Position, which means on your left side, facing the same direction you are.
2. Fold most of the leash into your right hand so there isn't much leash between your hand and his collar. You want it to be very short, not hanging in a loose loop.

3. Place your left hand in front of your dog's face, about six inches from his eyes, your palm open and facing him, your fingers pointing down. This hand signal suggests to your dog that you want him to remain where he is.

   At the same time, say, "Stay." Say it only once. Say it crisply. Your voice shouldn't go UP at the end—don't say "Stay?" as though you're begging him.

4. Take one small step forward with your RIGHT foot. It's furthest from your dog, so harder for him to see it move. If you stepped forward with your left foot, he might follow your leg motion and try to walk with you.

5. After your one step forward with your right foot, pivot to face your dog so you're standing only a few inches in front of him. AS you're taking this one step and pivoting, raise the leash over your dog's head so it's slightly taut. Slightly! Don't strangle your dog! It should be just snug enough to suggest to him that he should hold his position even though YOU'RE moving.

   If he should start to stand up, don't repeat the word "Stay." Dogs connect the word they hear with the action they are performing at that moment. You don't want him to connect the word "Stay" with the action of moving!

   Instead, say nothing—just be very quick with the leash, tugging it upward and slightly backward (toward his hindquarters) in an attempt to check him before he gets up. The goal is to keep him in position so that he never makes it all the way to his feet.

   If you're too slow and he does make it all the way to his feet, try not to move your own feet. Just hold his front end in position with the tight leash, reach over his back from your position in front of him, and push his hind end back into a sit so he's sitting in the same place he started. Then remove your hand from his rear end and continue to hold the leash slightly taut over his head.

If he tries to lie down instead, again be very quick and check him with the leash BEFORE he goes down. If you're too slow, you'll have to use the leash or your hands to pull him back up and replace him in the sitting position.

> 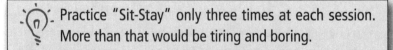 If he keeps breaking position again and again, add a firm "Ah-ah!" AS he is breaking. Make your tug on the leash sharper and your push on his hindquarters sterner.

6. Aim for your dog to hold his Sit-Stay for ten straight seconds. Count in your head: one one-thousand, two one-thousand, etc. Each time you have to correct him, start your count again.

7. When he has held his position for ten seconds, pivot back to his side. Use the slightly taut leash over his head to help him hold his position. Dogs often get excited when they see you coming back—but he must hold his position!

8. When you get back to his side, pause for five more seconds, so that he learns not to misinterpret your return as a cue to get up. If he does get up, just reposition him. Say nothing. Count to five seconds again, then praise him mildly (so he doesn't get too excited). "Good stay. Good." If he gets up when you praise him, just reposition him. Praise him mildly again.

9. Finally, when he is holding position for your praise, you can release him with a cheerful "Okay!"

> Practice "Sit-Stay" only three times at each session. More than that would be tiring and boring.

Each day, add another five to ten seconds to your count so that by the end of the week he is holding for about a minute. Also begin to relax the leash so you aren't holding it over his head as a reminder to hold position. Finally, back a step or two away from him—but don't go all the way to the end of the leash just yet.

Don't try to rush your dog through Sit-Stay training!

For example, don't push your dog to hold a Sit-Stay for a full minute on the very first day, thinking smugly that he is a fast-learning wonder dog who doesn't need to practice.

PRACTICE is what makes a dog rock-solid on the Sit-Stay. Like the concert pianist who faithfully practices simple finger exercises for years, even when he could do them in his sleep, a dog who practices short sit stays every day will end up much better trained.

Advanced Sit-Stay

Can your dog do these four things?

1. Hold a Sit-Stay for about a minute?
2. Hold a Sit-Stay even after you've returned to his side?
3. Hold a Sit-Stay even while you're praising him?
4. Hold a Sit-Stay until you release him with "Okay"?
5. Have you been practicing every day for a full week?

Yes? Then let's make it more interesting for both of you!

Circle around him

Instead of returning to his side via a simple pivot, circle around him counterclockwise. In other words, walk behind him and return to his right side from the rear.

The first few times you try this, hold the leash slightly taut above his head as you go around him, to remind him not to move. Otherwise he may try to turn with you, to see where you're going. With a medium to large dog, you might even place your left hand on his head as you're going by him, to help hold him in position.

If he turns his head to watch you, that's fine, but he mustn't swivel his body around to follow you.

Add distractions

Remember the distractions you used to "proof" your dog when he was learning WAIT (Word #32)?

Time for those distractions again!

Instead of standing still, walk back and forth in front of him. Or circle around him as though returning to your position beside him—but don't stop; make a full circle until you're back in front again. Cough. Laugh. Hum. Whistle a happy tune. Recite a poem. Do a few knee bends or jumping jacks.

After a few days of these simple distractions, is your dog still holding his Sit-Stay? Great! Have one of your kids walk by, bouncing a ball. Have one of your kids run by. Have one of your kids skip rope.

Be fair! Instruct your child not to call your dog, not to even look at the dog. Distractions, you see, should be normal things that might go on in your house or yard while your dog happens to be holding a Sit-Stay. You don't want to tease your dog by staring at him or by deliberately encouraging him to break.

Increase distance

After a week of distractions while you're standing right in front of your dog, move to the end of the leash and repeat the distractions.

If your dog breaks his Sit-Stay while you're at the end of the leash, go back to him to correct him. Don't try to correct him from the end of the leash. You'll only end up pulling him **toward** you.

Especially don't call out, "Stay!" when you see him starting to move. He should never hear this word when he's in the process of moving!

Instead, let him experience **the consequences of moving**, which means you say "Ah-ah!" as he is breaking, then you rush at him, grab him, and firmly reposition him in his original spot—the exact same spot.

This is a good time to emphasize that you should not stare at your dog when practicing "Stay." If you meet his eyes, he may think you're inviting him to come to you. Or he may feel uncomfortable under your scrutiny and try to avoid your gaze by lying down or walking away.

So look to the right of your dog. Look to the left. Look up and count the dust bunnies on the ceiling or the clouds in the sky. Rely on your peripheral (corner-of-your-eye) vision to keep track of your dog so you can quickly correct him if necessary.

Increase time

Begin increasing time, slowly, from a minute to two minutes, then three minutes. That's plenty long enough for sitting still.

Finally, drop the leash

The complete Sit-Stay program should take about a month to accomplish. Remember, if you rush through it, your dog will never be as solid as a dog who got to practice every day for the full month.

In the end, your goal is to be able to walk around the room doing normal household chores for three minutes while your dog holds his Sit-Stay. What a fine dog!

> If you need your dog to stay put for longer than three minutes, leave him in a lying down position. It's much more comfortable than sitting.

"What's the difference between Wait and Stay?"

Excellent question!

WAIT means "Don't cross a specific boundary." You use "Wait" when you don't want your dog to pass through a doorway or gate, or enter a room, or go up or down a flight of stairs—until you say so.

The boundary must be **clear** to your dog. In other words, he must be able to **see** the difference between "here" and "there." For example, a physical marker such as a door frame, or gate posts, or stairs. Or an obvious change of footing such as vinyl floor to carpet, or grass to concrete.

> With "Wait," as long as your dog doesn't cross the boundary, you don't care whether he stands, sits, lies down, or wanders around on his side of the boundary. He simply can't cross it.

STAY means "Hold an exact position." You put your dog in a specific place and position, and he must stay in that place and position.

If you put him in a sitting position, he has to stay sitting in that exact place. He can't lie down, or stand up, or move two feet to the right.

As you can see, "Stay" is much stricter than "Wait." Sometimes you need that strictness. For example, you may want your dog to sit and stay so the vet can examine his ears. It won't do for your dog to suddenly stand up, or flop onto his side, or wander around the examining room.

> When you need your dog to sit or lie down or stand still in one particular spot, that's when you use "Stay."

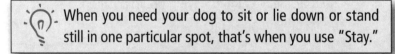

Emergency Down (with hand signal)

There's one final Down exercise to teach your dog.

- It's impressive.
- It will wow your friends.
- It could save your dog's life.

Suppose your dog gets away from you at the worst possible time—you're downtown and the leash breaks or he pulls it out of your hand. He runs across the street. You call him. He turns to come back to you. But there is a car coming.

> Sometimes "Come!" isn't the best word to use to gain control of your dog. Sometimes you just want your dog to stop dead in his tracks—and stay there until you arrive.

Those are times for the **Emergency Down**.

You shout, "Down!" You raise your right arm high in the air, a signal clearly visible from afar. Your dog drops like a stone to the ground and stays put while the car whizzes by.

Now, is that impressive, or what? Do you see the value of such an absolute control word?

Four steps in teaching the Emergency Down

Step #1 of the Emergency Down

1. Put a handful of treats in your pocket, and with your dog on leash, wander around your house or yard. When his attention is elsewhere, say, when he is sniffing something, stop walking and say his name clearly, "Jake!"

Again, sound familiar? This is the same first step for teaching your dog his name, and also to come when called. When he hears his name, he should turn to look at you.

2. When your dog looks at you in response to his name, raise your right arm high in the air—a sharp, definitive gesture, all five fingers pointing firmly toward the sky and your palm facing your dog.

3. At the same time, say, "Down!" and take a large fast step toward him. Grasp the leash just below the clasp and stop him in his tracks before he can take any steps toward you. Tug the leash downward to encourage him to lie down. If necessary, push down on his shoulders—but this shouldn't be necessary if you've already taught him to lie down on command. (Word #28.)

    The goal is to keep him as close to his original position as possible. Remember the example where your dog was across the street and a car was coming? If you gave him the down signal and he walked several feet toward you before lying down, he might be under the wheels of the car!

> So be picky when teaching this word—your dog should lie down as quickly as possible and as close to his original position as possible.

4. Once he is down, praise him softly, "Good boy" and caution him, "Stay." Step back to the end of the leash and wait about ten seconds.

5. Then return to him and release him: "Okay!" Now praise him lavishly and cavort around with him to let him know he has just accomplished a wonderful thing.

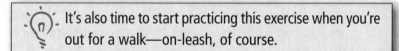

This can be a stressful exercise for a dog, so don't practice several Emergency Downs in a row. One is enough. Then play with your dog and don't try another one until later.

Step #2 in teaching the Emergency Down

After a week of using your hand on the leash to stop him in his tracks and help guide him down, it's time for him to start assuming this responsibility himself.

Give him the down signal and tell him, "Down!" If he keeps moving toward you, use the leash to bounce him firmly back to his original position—where he was standing when you gave him the command—and then use the leash, just as firmly, to put him down.

These are corrections now, not gentle guidance.

It's also time to start practicing this exercise when you're out for a walk—on-leash, of course.

Step #3 in teaching the Emergency Down

We're going to get more advanced now!
1. Put your dog in a Sit-Stay and go to the end of the leash. Raise your arm in the down signal and tell him, "Down!"
2. If he lies down immediately (within one second), praise him quietly—don't get him excited—and caution him to stay put. "Good. Stay." Wait ten seconds to allow him to settle, then return to his side as though completing a regular Sit-Stay exercise. Release him with "Okay!" and praise him vociferously!

What if he didn't immediately lie down when you told him to? Take a large fast step toward him, grasp the leash just below the snap, and firmly tug him down. Step back to the end of the leash, wait ten seconds, then return to his side and release him as above.

3. Play with your dog for a few minutes, then place him in another Sit-Stay. But this time, CALL HIM. "Jake, come!" He should do this part flawlessly!

4. Play with your dog for another few minutes, then place him in one more Sit-Stay. This time, return to his side without either downing him or calling him.

> You're teaching your dog to pay close attention to your words! By varying what you say and do, he must listen carefully, rather than trying to anticipate.

Also vary your time and distance. One time, wait thirty seconds before you down him or call him or return to his side. The next time, wait sixty seconds. Then a short fifteen-second wait. Practice on a regular leash and a 20-foot leash.

Step #4 in teaching the Emergency Down

With your dog's leash attached, take him outside in your yard and drop your end of the leash. Maneuver yourself so that he is about ten feet away from you. Watch for him to look up and make eye contact with you. At that moment, raise your right arm high in the air and call in a commanding voice, "Down!"

If he goes down immediately, caution him, "Stay!" Walk toward him, repeating your caution to "Stay. Good. Stay." When you reach him, crouch down and pet him and praise him softly. Make sure he stays down as you do so. Then release him with, "Okay!" and really, really praise him!

If he doesn't go down immediately—if he just stands there looking at you—repeat, "Down!" in a firm voice. Your arm should still be in the air giving the down signal. If he responds to your stronger tone, follow through as described above, as though he had gone down properly the first time. You're giving him some leeway while he's still learning.

If he didn't go down on either the first or second try, walk purposefully out to get him. He will probably realize that you're coming to correct him and he may try to evade you. Remember, don't speak to him or chase him—just track him down until you can get hold of the leash.

Lead him all the way back to the spot where he was originally standing when you told him to lie down. Use the leash to put him down there, and tell him, "Stay."

Then walk back to where YOU were originally standing when you first told him to lie down. Wait ten seconds for him to settle, and return to him. Crouch down and pet him and praise him softly. Make sure he stays down. Then release him with, "Okay!"

Practice this exercise every day until your dog is rock-solid. Then replace the dragging leash with a shorter hand-hold (discussed in Chapter 1). A hand-hold gives you something to latch onto if you still need to catch and correct him.

"OFF" (the furniture)

Word #35: "Off"

Some owners don't want their dogs on the furniture, especially if the dog is huge, or sheds a lot, or slobbers and drools.

But certain breeds, especially toy dogs and sighthounds, love being on the furniture. Toy dogs like to be up high where they can see better and feel protected. Greyhound type dogs, with their smooth hair and thin sensitive skin, are most comfortable when snuggled into soft cushions.

 In my opinion, if you choose one of these breeds, it's unkind to keep him off all the furniture.

Some owners find a middle ground. They don't mind their dog on some furniture, but they have one or two special pieces on which they would prefer their dog not sleep. If you're in this camp, simply use "No" whenever you catch your dog on the forbidden piece of furniture.

I'll tell you why. There are some things you want your dog **never** to do. That's what "No" is for. If you **never** want your dog on a specific piece of furniture, tell him "No" whenever he gets up there and chase him off.

BUT...

If your dog is **usually** allowed on the furniture, but you want him to stay off it **temporarily**, you should use a different word.

For example, suppose a guest who isn't comfortable with your dog is sitting on the couch. Or perhaps you're sitting on the couch with a plate of food on your lap. Or maybe you're lying on the couch because you're sick. Or perhaps you have important papers strewn across the couch.

These are all examples of when you might not want your dog on the couch. Since he is usually allowed up there, he would be confused if you suddenly told him "No."

That's why you need a different word—one that means "Sorry, big guy, but the couch is off limits for the moment."

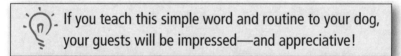 That word is "Off." Combine it with a natural waving motion of your hand and make sure he does get off, even if you have to guide him by the collar.

My dog Buffy lies on the couch with us when we're watching TV. But when food appears, she is not allowed to remain on the couch. We've been so consistent in telling her "Off" whenever food appears that she jumps off as soon as she sees the dinner plates in our hands.

If you teach this simple word and routine to your dog, your guests will be impressed—and appreciative!

"Shoo" (Be somewhere else!)

Word #36: "Shoo"

Some people prefer "Shoo" while others prefer "Git" or "Go on" or "Move." It's hard for me to describe exactly where this word should be used, but you will use it, I promise you. When it fits the situation, it comes quickly to mind as the perfect word.

For example, I don't allow my dog Buffy in the Bird Room where I raise canaries. She is a gentle dog who wouldn't hurt them, but they don't know that and her presence makes them nervous.

So she accompanies me to the Bird Room door, where I remind her, "Wait." She stops obediently, waiting in the hall—sometimes peeking into the room, sometimes lying down just outside the door, sometimes wandering away for a drink of water, always coming back to check on my whereabouts.

But occasionally she sneaks into the Bird Room, just a few steps. She stands there, watching. When I spot her, I wave my hand at her in a rapid shooing motion. "Buffy, git!" I say. "G'won!" And she scampers out.

Teaching it is simple. Pronounce the word crisply, combine it with a natural shooing motion of your hand, and make sure your dog moves away from whatever you want him to move away from, even if you have to guide him by the collar.

- Dog standing in the garden. Crushing flowers! "Shoo!"
- Dog wandering into the garage. Antifreeze in there! "Shoo!"
- Dog begging at the table. "Shoo!"
- Dog poking his head into the bedroom. You and your spouse are engaged in...um... "Shoo!"

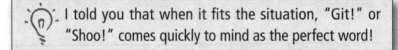

I told you that when it fits the situation, "Git!" or "Shoo!" comes quickly to mind as the perfect word!

"Go lie down" (when you're busy)

Word #37: "Go Lie Down"

This phrase is a combination of "Shoo" and "Down"—you want your dog to move a distance away from you and lie down. Unlike plain old "Shoo," where your dog simply needs to take himself elsewhere, "Go lie down" requires him to assume a specific position.

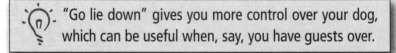

"Go lie down" gives you more control over your dog, which can be useful when, say, you have guests over.

Once your dog has learned both "Shoo" and "Down," it's an easy matter to combine the two.

1. Point or wave your hand toward a corner of the room and tell him, "Go lie down."
2. Lead him by the collar (Gently! You're teaching him a phrase he doesn't yet know!).
3. Tell him "Down" when you reach the corner, and see that he does so.

One problem with "Go lie down"

There is one aspect of "Go lie down" that does present a problem. You might remember, when we were teaching your dog the Long Down, that you were cautioned NEVER to put your dog in a Long Down and then let yourself get distracted. Do you remember why?

That's right. If you get distracted, he will break the Long Down and wander away on his own, without waiting for you to release him with "Okay!"

Well, that's what can happen with "Go lie down" as well. If you send your dog across the room to lie down, and then forget he's there, he will soon stand up and walk away.

Not good for your Leader–Follower relationship!

> So…I suggest using "Go lie down" only when you're sure you will remember to keep an eye on your dog and will release him within 30 minutes.

Chapter 13

Walking and Exercise

The best collars and leashes

I DO NOT recommend choke collars.

A **choke collar** applies sudden pressure concentrated at a specific point on your dog's neck. A choke collar can damage your dog's windpipe. The choking sensation frightens many dogs. And choke collars can tear the hair around your dog's neck.

Choke collars are sometimes called "slip collars" or "training collars" but they're definitely not needed for training and I don't recommend them.

Instead, I recommend a **flat buckle collar** of nylon or leather. It simply buckles around your dog's neck. Most dogs never need anything more.

For small- to medium-sized dogs, the buckle collar can be ⅝ inch to ¾ inch wide and single-layer. For large, strong dogs, you might want a collar that's an inch wide and double-layer.

For toy dogs I like the Top Paw® **Sunburst collar**, which is ⅜ inch wide and made of very soft fabric that allows the buckle "to seek its own hole" so it's completely adjustable for a perfect fit. It comes in lengths as short as 8 inches.

For longhaired dogs, instead of a flat collar, you may prefer a **rolled collar**, which is made of narrow, rounded leather that doesn't squash the hair.

A **harness** is no good for training because the leash connects to the middle of your dog's back, which means you can't guide his head. To teach many words, you must be able to guide your dog's head.

 However, a **Y-shaped** harness is recommended for **walking** toy dogs, who often have delicate windpipes. A Y-harness doesn't encircle the throat. The straps come down from each shoulder to form a Y on the chest. The tail of the Y goes down between the front legs, where it eventually meets up with the strap that wraps around the stomach.

Unfortunately, a Y-harness is hard to find. Most harnesses in pet stores have a strap that wraps around the throat—which defeats the whole reason for getting a harness in the first place!

My favorite leash is made of **cotton webbing**, which feels like flexible cloth. Usually it's olive green or black. Unfortunately, a cotton web leash can be hard to find. Most leashes at pet stores are made of nylon, which can be stiff and a bit sharp in your hands. **Leather** leashes are nice but very stiff unless well-oiled or until well-worn.

Chain leashes are terrible—don't use them for anything. Chain leashes are cold, they clank and clatter against your dog, and they're only as strong as their weakest link.

A **retractable** leash is too clunky and awkward for training, but okay for walks. Just don't abuse it. I've seen people allow their dog to roam to the end of a 16-foot retractable leash in a crowd of people. The dog could approach people who didn't want to be approached, jump on them, and tangle the leash around their legs.

Use retractable leashes sensibly. You can allow full leash length in open fields or parks or along quiet roads. But when people or other dogs are  nearby, or when you're walking near a road with traffic, shorten the leash so your dog is close beside you and fully under control.

 PetsMart stores (and online at *www.petsmart.com*) have many of the collars and leashes I recommend.

Teach your dog to walk without pulling

Word #38: "Go For A Walk?"

As you might guess, this is a beloved phrase that dogs learn very quickly! All you need do is say it in a happy tone, then follow up immediately by clipping on his leash and taking him for a walk.

Make sure there's no delay! Don't ask your dog if he wants to go for a walk, then get bogged down checking the weather, choosing the right jacket, grabbing a snack, visiting the bathroom, and hunting around for your dog's leash.

Make your preparations ahead of time. Find out what the weather is and decide which jacket you're going to wear. Put a snack in your pocket. Go to the bathroom. Check to see that his leash is in the closet where you thought it was.

THEN ask your dog, "Want to go for a WALK?" and whisk him outside right away.

> :bulb: When introducing new words, you must deliver on your promises very quickly so that he makes the connection. If the phone rings on your way out, let the answering machine get it. You're going for a walk!

Word #39: "Where's Your Leash?"

After your dog shows that he understands "Want to go for a walk?" (by dancing around with excitement), add one more level of complexity: "Jake, where's your LEASH?"

As with any other object word, you teach "leash" by repeatedly holding up the leash, showing it to your dog, and emphasizing the word. Put it in its rightful place—always the same place—a hook on the wall, table by the door, shelf, drawer, or closet. Now encourage your dog to run to it: "Where's your LEASH? Find your LEASH!"

Run to the leash yourself. Make a big production out of showing it to your dog. "Yay! Good leash!" With dogs (and small children), melodrama is very effective.

If your dog likes to hold things in his mouth, you can try offering him the leash and encouraging him to carry it to the front door. Otherwise, just be satisfied if he has obviously made a connection between the sound *leash* and its matching object.

Now take him for a walk!

How to go for a walk

Once you're actually out walking, your dog should walk politely. Nobody wants their dog to pull and lunge and gasp on the leash like *The Hound of the Baskervilles.*

Why pulling is bad

- Pulling is uncomfortable for the person holding the leash. Even if YOU can hold onto your pulling dog, how could anyone else take him for a walk if they ever had to?

- A pulling dog is being disrespectful. You are on this walk, too. You, in fact, are supposed to be the leader who sets the pace of the walk. A pulling dog hardly even knows, or cares, that you're there. He is not showing a good follower attitude.

- A pulling dog is not practicing self-control. He's acting impulsively and focusing on immediate self-gratification. Teaching your dog self-control is important if you want a well-behaved dog.

- A pulling dog is representing his breed poorly in public. You don't want people shaking their heads at the (insert your dog's breed) who can't even walk on a leash. Whichever breed we choose to raise and train, we need to do our part to show the public that this breed is capable of good manners—and that WE are capable of training him.

Does your dog have to "heel" when walking?

There are two ways you can go for a walk with your dog.

1. You can have him **heel** very close beside your left leg. This is a very formal way of walking. It's what you see in AKC obedience competitions.

2. The more informal way of walking is to let your dog wander a little in front of you or off to either side—just as long as he doesn't pull on the leash.

Right now we're going to learn this second way of walking, the informal way. (We'll learn the more formal heeling later.)

Honestly, the informal way of walking is much more useful because most of the time, when you take your dog for a walk, you want him to enjoy himself. You want him to have some freedom on the leash so he can sniff around and even relieve himself if necessary. You don't want him to be so concerned about maintaining an exact position beside you that he can't even enjoy the scenery.

You just don't want him to pull!

How to handle pulling on the leash

The natural tendency when your dog starts to pull on the leash is for you to pull backward, trying to hold him back.

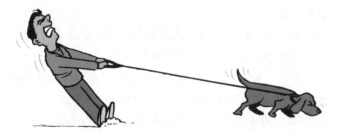

But if your dog is pulling in one direction and you're pulling in the other direction, how can there possibly be a loose leash between you? You're both pulling!

No, the key to counteracting pulling is a clever technique called the **Quick Tug and Relax**.

Here's how you do the Quick Tug and Relax:

1. Move your hand forward—**very, very quickly!** That's right, move your hand **toward** your pulling dog. This quick movement in the same direction as your dog is pulling will create a tiny bit of slack in the leash.

2. Now move your hand backward. The instant you have that tiny bit of slack, **very, very quickly**, TUG your hand **backward**. Don't pull the leash steadily—TUG it.

    This sudden forward-backward movement will throw your dog off-balance—and if you've done it with just the right amount of force for your dog's size and personality, it should propel him a few inches in your direction, which creates a nice loose leash.

3. Now relax your hand.

As you do all three steps, **keep walking.** If your dog surges forward again and tightens the leash, repeat the three steps:

- Hand forward—fast.
- Hand backward—TUG.
- Relax.

If your dog KEEPS pulling

If you've been doing the Quick Tug and Relax repeatedly, yet your dog continues to pull, add these two steps:

4. As you do your backward TUG, **turn and walk briskly in the opposite direction.** Your dog will find himself behind you and will need to hurry to catch up with you. (Doesn't it feel more satisfying to have him behind you and scrambling to catch up, rather than pulling ahead?)

5. After taking only a few steps in the new direction, suddenly reverse yourself again so that now you're walking in your original direction.

Again your dog will find himself trailing behind and will have to scramble to catch up. It won't be long before he realizes that for some bizarre reason, whenever he tightens the leash, it causes you to walk in the opposite direction! How odd!

Your frequent changes in direction will hinder him from progressing on his walk—and those leash tugs make him darned uncomfortable. To avoid these problems, he will begin taking on the responsibility for keeping the leash loose himself. That's right. You'll soon notice that whenever he feels himself getting too far ahead, he will hasten to slow down before you have a chance to do one of your cuckoo direction changes!

You'll probably also notice him occasionally glancing over his shoulder to make sure you're still there. Before, you see, when he was pulling, he didn't need to look at you in order to know where you were—he could feel you at the other end of the taut leash. Now, with the leash loose, he must actually pay some attention to your whereabouts by checking back with his eyeballs.

 Your dog **should** be paying attention to your whereabouts. It's a simple matter of respect!

Very strong pullers: a special case

For very strong dogs who pull so hard on the leash that the Quick Tug and Relax doesn't work for them, a **prong collar** is the next step up.

A prong collar works somewhat like a choke collar in that the collar tightens around your

dog's neck when you tug on the leash. However, unlike a choke collar, a prong collar has rounded, blunt-edged "prongs" that spread pressure **evenly** around your dog's neck, and just as importantly, the collar can only tighten so far—never enough to choke him.

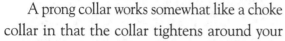 A prong collar has been referred to as **power steering** because you only have to give a gentle tug and most dogs respond quickly.

How to put on a prong collar

1. Grasp one prong with one hand and its neighbor prong with the other hand.
2. Pinch one of these prongs together until it disengages from its neighbor.
3. Move your hands apart to open the collar into a U-shape.
4. Place it around your dog's neck, up high behind his ears.
5. Slip the two prongs back together, which closes the collar around his neck. The collar should be snug enough that it doesn't slide. If you need to make it smaller, take it off and remove a prong. If you need to make it larger, buy additional prongs or move up to the next size collar.
6. Arrange the collar so the prongs are on TOP of the neck. The section of the collar without the prongs goes under the neck, where the skin is most sensitive.

7.   Slide the ring that the leash attaches to onto the RIGHT side of your dog's neck, and clip on the leash.

> Most dogs who need a prong collar need it only for a very short time, to settle them down and bring their rambunctiousness under control. Then you can try the regular buckle collar again.

Alternatively, some dogs who don't respond well to a regular buckle collar do well with a **head halter**. Gentle Leader® and Halti are popular brands.

The theory is that where the head goes, the rest of the body follows. For some dogs, these halters work almost magically, turning a hyperactive puller into a calm follower with very little effort on your part. For other dogs, these halters don't work at all—some dogs will fight the pressure on their face and become panicky.

Head halters require different leash-handling techniques than the ones we've talked about in this chapter. Gentle Leader® offers a video that shows you how to use the halter and handle the leash.

Things your dog shouldn't do on a walk

- He shouldn't snuffle constantly along the ground looking for things to eat. Tug firmly on the leash and tell him "Stop that" or "Leave it."
- He shouldn't bark or growl at passersby or other dogs. (We'll cover this in Chapter 15: The Sociable Dog.)
- He shouldn't stop to lift his leg on every bush, fire hydrant, and telephone pole.

Dogs who try to pee against every vertical object they pass are obsessed with "marking territory." Leaving their scent for other dogs to smell makes them feel bossy and self-important. This attitude often carries over into other areas of their life, such as ignoring your rules or bickering with other dogs. Unneutered males, especially those with dominant personalities, are the biggest offenders when it comes to compulsive marking. But some neutered males do it, too, and even females, spayed or not, may do it.

Don't allow compulsive marking

Once your dog has peed a few times, that's enough. If he tries to keep stopping, just tell him "Ah-ah, let's go!" and keep towing him along at a steady clip.

He'll soon learn that he must relieve himself as soon as you go out rather than holding it for distribution throughout the walk. Having taken care of business early on, he can relax and look around during the walk, instead of lunging for every blade of grass and turning the walk into a compulsive pee-fest to show everyone how tough he is.

Teach your dog to find his way home

Word #40: "Go Home"

No one wants to imagine this happening … but suppose your dog somehow gets out of your house. He wanders along the street, by some miracle avoiding being hit by a car. Then he takes a good look around and decides that the big wide world is no place for this little doggie!

He wants to go home. Does he know his way home?

Many dogs seldom see their house from the sidewalk. How can they find their way home if they get out?

Sure, some dogs might backtrack their own scent home. Others might wander around aimlessly and accidentally end up near their house, where they might pick up their scent or their owner's scent on the gate or driveway.

But your dog will have a much better chance of finding his way home if he learns what his house and yard look like from the street—and how to find them when he's down the street or even on a nearby street.

Teach your dog to find his way home

1. Choose a door to designate as **home.** As you're leaving the house with your dog, on leash, place one of his favorite treats at the **home door**, perhaps on the door mat. Make sure he sees you do it—make a big show of it!

2. Lead him a very short distance away, just down the steps or down the walk.

3. Turn and point him in the right direction, and encourage him, "Go home!" Then RUN to the door with him—let him pull on the leash all he wants for this exercise—and point out the treat so he can gobble it up.

    With such an incentive, he'll master this phrase very quickly!

4. After he has learned the concept and dashes immediately to the door every time, drop the leash—as long as your dog is reliable with "Come!" and as long as you're not on a busy street. Let him drag the leash to the front door while you trot along behind him.

5. Now it's only a matter of getting farther and farther away and showing him the way home from different directions.

    Don't dawdle once you've told him "Go home!" Don't let him stop to sniff anything. Get home fast so he makes the connection. Encourage him all the way, "Go HOME! Home, home!" If he tries to turn up the wrong street or driveway or walkway, use the leash to check him gently, "Ah-ah, no-no. Go HOME!"

> Always have a treat waiting for him at home, or give him one from your pocket when you arrive.

And if, heaven forbid, your dog ever does get out, prop open his **home door** so he can enter the house. You don't want him finding his way home to a closed door and wandering away again. (Of course, if you have other pets, confine them in other rooms while the home door is open.)

How much exercise your dog needs

Every morning before work, Roger took his dog Jake for a five-minute walk. They walked down the driveway to the corner, where Jake lifted his leg on a telephone pole. Then back home again. After supper, Kathy took Jake once around the block.

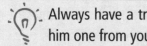

So when the vet suggested that Jake's high energy level and frequent misbehavior might call for more exercise, Roger and Kathy exclaimed, with indignation, "What?? He gets plenty of exercise!!"

Energetic dogs require **vigorous** daily exercise. That doesn't mean a leisurely walk around the block. It means several miles, or a good hour or so, of **brisk** exercise each and every day.

Now, if you happen to have two or more dogs who romp and play with each other in the house and yard, they will burn off energy through wrestling and chase games. Add some brisk sessions of ball-playing or stick-fetching, and they're pretty much all set.

If you don't have multiple dogs who play with each other, YOU need to exercise your high-energy dog. Otherwise he will become restless and hyperactive and will try to release his pent-up energy through destructive chewing, digging, and barking.

Many dogs described as hyperactive or destructive are simply dogs who aren't getting enough exercise.

A hyperactive, destructive dog is trying to vent bottled-up energy. You cannot fix this kind of misbehavior with training. You must provide more exercise.

Not like this!

Many breeds were never intended to be pets. They were developed for working purposes and have inherited instincts for high energy. A breed with strong working instincts may bounce off the walls because, instead of providing him with a good hour or more of brisk daily exercise, you're walking him around the block or assuming that he'll exercise himself if you simply stick him outside alone, in the back yard.

Examples of active working breeds include Airedales, Australian Shepherds, Beagles, Border Collies, Brittanys, Dalmatians, Giant Schnauzers, Jack Russell Terriers, German Shorthaired Pointers, Irish Setters, Siberian Huskies, Springer Spaniels, Vizslas, Weimaraners, and plenty of other breeds.

If you can meet their exercise needs, these breeds are fine. If you can't, the dog deserves another home that CAN, and you need to choose a different breed.

Don't try to fit a square dog into a round family! Both Dog and Family will be unhappy.

Exercise suggestions for active breeds

- Walking. For 45–90 minutes, once or twice a day.
- Free running. In a safe, enclosed area.
- Fetch games. With balls, sticks, or Frisbees®.
- Playing with other dogs.
- Doggy obstacle course. See Chapter 19.
- Swimming.
- Carting, sledding, weight-pulling.
- Hiking/backpacking.

Caution! These exercise suggestions are for healthy, normally-shaped adult dogs. Puppies and adolescents have very different exercise requirements, or you may damage their bones and joints. Senior dogs, overweight dogs, toy dogs, giant dogs, and flat-faced dogs also have special exercise requirements.

 My health book, *Dog Care Wisdom: 11 Things You Must Do Right To Keep Your Dog Healthy and Happy,* includes specific exercise programs for all these different ages, sizes, and shapes.

Chapter 14
The Quiet Dog

Dogs who bark too much at the door

Does your dog bark when someone comes to the door? Good for him! Watchfulness is a natural canine trait.

But too much of a good thing can be...annoying.

- Does your dog keep barking even after you open the door?
- Do you find yourself trying to read your visitor's lips over the racket your dog is making?
- Do you need to grab at your dog and try to shush him while also trying to pay attention to your visitor?

Excessive barking at visitors must be stopped

If your dog keeps barking even after you've answered the door...

- he is taking it upon himself to decide whether a visitor is a threat or not, when he should be leaving that decision up to the pack leader, which is supposed to be you.
- OR he is simply barking mindlessly, displaying no self-control whatsoever.

Either way, this is not the kind of dog you want.

On-Off Switch–"Speak" and "Quiet"

Once your dog has sounded the alarm, he must turn the situation over to you. If YOU decide the person at the door is harmless (even welcome), your dog must accept your judgment and close his mouth.

To do that, he needs an On-Off Switch. You will teach your dog to bark on command, and to STOP barking on command. This allows him to use his voice sometimes, which is natural for him to do.

Word #41: "Speak"

What makes your dog bark? The doorbell ringing? Vacuum cleaner turning on? A jingling collar that suggests another dog passing by?

How to teach your dog to speak

1. If you have a helper, have him or her do whatever makes your dog bark, i.e. ring the doorbell, turn on the vacuum cleaner, or jingle a collar. If you don't have any assistance, obviously you'll have to do this yourself.

2. Your dog will probably be barking already, so encourage him to keep doing so: "Speak! Good boy! Speak!" Add a hand signal by making a "talking mouth" with your hand, i.e. moving your fingers up and down so the four fingers touch the thumb, then open again, then close again, like a fast-talking mouth (gab-gab-gab). Keep him excited. Make speaking on command a really fun experience!

   If he is reluctant to cooperate, sometimes barking yourself ("Speak! Ruff! Ruff!") will motivate your dog to chime in. You might even tie him to a post or have someone hold his leash while you stand just out of range with a tempting toy or treat and encourage him to "Speak!" Such playful teasing is okay in the beginning. Don't worry, you won't need to keep doing it once your dog learns the word.

Word #42: "Quiet" or ("No Bark")

1. Make sure your dog has his leash or hand-hold on. Have a friend come to the door and knock or ring the bell.
2. Your dog will probably rush the door, barking. Go with him. Even though he is already barking, TURN HIM ON with "Good boy! Speak!"
3. Then TURN HIM OFF. "Enough! Quiet." Your dog is already familiar with "Enough" (Word #10) meaning "No More," so he may stop barking. If he doesn't, correct him with a spray of water from a squirt gun, or a sideways snap of the leash, or a commercial beeping device like The Barker Breaker® by Amtek, which produces a loud high-pitched sound that makes many dogs scramble away from whatever behavior they were engaging in. (Just be forewarned that it's loud and shrill for human ears, too!) Visit *www.amtekpet.com* for more information.

   Correct your dog as many times as necessary until he stops barking. (Your friend outside will just have to be patient.)
4. When your dog is finally quiet, open the door and let your friend in. If your dog jumps on your friend, use the leash or hand-hold to tug him off. "No! Stop that!"

   Your friend can also correct jumping by refusing to reach down and touch your jumping dog. In fact, he can bring his knee up quickly so your dog bumps against it. Only when your dog has four feet on the floor should your friend reach down and pet him.

Stopping barking when you're not home

- Does your dog stand at the window and bark at the neighbors when they're outside in their own yard?
- Does he bark at the neighbor's dog?
- Does he bark at passersby on the sidewalk?

- Does he bark when other neighborhood dogs bark?
- Does he bark at the garbage truck, the UPS truck, or other vehicles that pull up anywhere on the street?

Now, if your dog offers a few woofs when these events occur, fine. He's being a good watchdog.

But if he barks for more than THIRTY SECONDS, he's a nuisance.

Yes, you read that right. Thirty seconds. A well-behaved dog does NOT disturb the neighbors. If my neighbor's dog were to bark on and on at me when I'm in my own yard, or if he barked at anything and everything that caught his attention, I would call Animal Control with no hesitation whatsoever.

Your neighbors have a right to peace and quiet in their own home and yard.

I'm serious about this. A dog who barks and barks is not a watchdog. He's The Dog Who Cried Wolf. No one even comes to their window to see what he's barking at any more. He's a sheer nuisance.

If this describes your dog, the first step in quieting him is to think about why he's barking so much.

WHY is your dog barking?

He may be barking at passersby because he's trying to chase them away from his territory. And you know what? In your dog's eyes, it works! If people walk by his house and he barks and they keep right on going, your barking dog believes he chased them away.

Or he may bark for the opposite reason—because he views passersby as potential playmates who might be encouraged to come closer with enthusiastic barking.

He may bark because he's trying to call you home. Such dogs usually have an unhealthy dependent relationship with you. They think they can't get through the day without you.

> Since you invariably DO come home at some point, your dog believes that his barking works. So each day he repeats it until "you finally hear him" and come home!

Other dogs try to call you home, too, but not because they miss you—rather, they've become accustomed to being the center of attention and they're annoyed that you're not there to entertain them.

> These are the same dogs who demand attention when you have guests over, or when you talk on the phone or hug your spouse.

Some dogs bark because they're not getting enough physical and mental exercise to tire them out. They're restless and bored and need to vent their energy.

And some dogs bark because they're **truly lonely**. Most dogs are sociable creatures who need the companionship of other sociable creatures in order to feel happy. You might try to convince yourself that your single dog is happy being left alone all day, because it makes you feel less guilty—but he isn't.

How to stop barking when you're not home

Block your dog's view of his territory. Pull the shades or drapes, or put other barriers between your dog and the outside world. Or leave him in a room without a view—or in an indoor pen. For short periods (no more than four hours!), you can leave him in a crate.

Muffle sounds from outside. Put on the TV, radio, or CD player. Let him listen to something peaceful and restful—classical music, soft jazz, or environmental/nature sounds. Don't leave him with hard rock or rap music, or with sitcoms. Loud, excitable, argumentative voices are stressful to listen to.

Encourage independence. Re-read Word #10: "Enough" to be sure you're not fostering a dependent relationship with your dog. He must learn how to stand on his own four feet and entertain himself without you always being there with him.

Don't allow demanding behaviors. Re-read **Don't Allow Demanding Behaviors** (Chapter 7) to be sure you're not allowing your dog to demand biscuits, or petting, or playtime. He must learn that he cannot order you around, which includes barking to demand that you come home.

Provide more exercise. Re-read **How Much Exercise Your Dog Needs** in Chapter 13. Many barking dogs are not getting enough exercise.

Stage corrective set-ups. This means leaving the house, lurking close by until you hear your dog barking, then charging back inside to correct him.

Get your dog a companion. If your dog must be alone for more than four hours a day, seriously consider getting him a canine companion. Most dogs are sociable creatures who need to be with other sociable creatures.

Of course, there are some dogs who are too aggressive to live safely with another dog. Similarly, some dogs are too old or frail or set in their ways, and might feel threatened by another dog usurping their position. But most normal, healthy dogs would love a carefully-chosen companion who complements their size and personality.

> **CAUTION!** If your dog is barking because he's lonely (because everyone at your house works or goes to school), **DO NOT GET A PUPPY** to keep him company.

A puppy will follow the lead of your older dog and soon you'll have TWO barking dogs! And puppies require far too much socialization, training, housebreaking, and companionship—sprinkled throughout the day in short bursts. Puppies belong in homes where someone is home most of the day.

No, for a lonely barking dog, go to the animal shelter or dog rescue group and choose an adult companion who is a calm, well-behaved NON-barker.

I'm assuming here that your dog is an INDOOR dog who is barking when he is INDOORS.

Stopping barking in outdoor dogs

If your dog is **outdoors** when he barks—especially if you're not home—you've got a MAJOR problem.

When an outdoor dog is barking, it's unfair to your neighbors to wait while you experiment with ideas such as blocking his view, increasing his exercise, etc., based on the hopes that his barking will stop. As you're futzing around with his environment to see what might work, he will still be disturbing the peace of other people.

As for getting him a companion to keep him company, forget it. TWO outdoor dogs who are barking are far worse than one.

> No, there is only one solution for outdoor barking: **BRING YOUR DOG INDOORS** whenever you leave the house. Period.

> But I wanted an outdoor dog!

Sorry. We don't always get what we want. If you want to be a responsible owner and a responsible neighbor, your barking dog cannot be an outdoor dog. That's life.

It's all for the best, anyway, because outdoor dogs are not happy.

Sorry to be so blunt, but that's how it is. Sled dogs and livestock guardians are okay with living outdoors because they're allowed to regularly perform the work they are genetically "hardwired" to do. They're willing to give up family life in order to "follow their genes" and work.

But if you want a dog as a family companion, only an indoor dog can fulfill this role. Dogs are sociable creatures who need to be close to their families—lounging in the same room, listening to conversations, waiting for you to come out of the bathroom, bringing toys to you, lying on the rug near the fire or television.

Dogs who spend most of their time outdoors are forced to stay "outside" their pack, living on the edge of it, never really immersed in day-to-day family life. An outdoor dog will never become the kind of well-behaved companion that an indoor dog can become.

> This book is intended for people who want a true family companion, whose intelligence and good behavior can be developed as fully as possible. That won't happen with an outdoor dog.

So if your dog is outdoors because a family member is allergic to him

...he needs a different home, and you need a different breed. Consult my dog buying guide: *How To Buy a Good Dog* for assistance with this.

If your dog is outdoors because he's too rambunctious

...you need to offer more exercise (and training) to calm him down. If he needs more exercise and training than you can provide, then he needs a different home and you need a different dog who CAN be happy with the amount of exercise and training you have to offer.

If your dog is outdoors because he's destructive or not housebroken

...you need to start crate training and housebreaking. Re-read Chapters 8 and 9. And at the risk of sounding like a broken record, if you don't have the time, or if you work all day (no dog can be crated all day), he needs a different home and you need a different dog who is already housebroken and well-behaved indoors.

Whatever you have to do, if you want a true family companion, bring your dog indoors or find him another home.

How to leave your dog home alone

"Jake, sweetie, Mummy and Daddy have to go out for awhile, okay? We're really sorry we have to leave you all by yourself. But we have to, Jake. Don't be mad and don't be scared—we'll come back, we promise! Be a good boy, okay? We love you, sweetheart, it will be okay, we'll be home soon!"

Ewww! Don't do this! When you have to leave your dog alone for a few hours, don't make a big emotional scene. A huge exit revs up your dog's nervous system and creates anxiety, which he will probably try to relieve through chewing or digging or barking. Instead:

1. Tire him out before you leave. Take him for a walk. Let him run in the yard. Throw a ball or toy for him to retrieve. Practice some obedience exercises.

2. A few minutes before you leave, take him outside to relieve himself.

3. Turn on soothing classical music or tune the TV to a local community station that plays pleasant elevator music.

4. If your dog will be in his crate while you're gone (no more than four hours!), put him in now. Give him a Nylabone® or heavy-duty Kong® toy to chew on.

5. Sit quietly in a chair for a few minutes, reading the paper or watching TV. When your dog is quiet and relaxed, get up from your chair and say, "Good boy, Jake. Wait here." Then leave. No fondling, no emotional good-byes, no lingering looks. Just leave matter-of-factly.

Similarly, when you come home

…don't burst in the door and overwhelm your dog with hugs and kisses and shrieks of glee.

Such a melodramatic entrance, after many quiet hours alone, is too stimulating for your dog's nervous system. He will soon begin to anticipate your homecoming long before you get home, and as he awaits the big emotional scene, he will become restless and anxious, which he will probably try to relieve through chewing or digging or barking. Instead:

1. Open the door and come in. Say calmly: "Hi, Jake."
2. **IGNORE HIM FOR A FULL THIRTY SECONDS**—whether he is loose in the house and jumping all around you, or whether he is in his crate.

    Hang up your jacket. Put your bags on the counter. Put away your purse. Don't pay any attention to your dog—don't even look at him. If he barks or whines or jumps on you, correct him with a quiet, matter-of-fact "No" or "Stop that."
3. When the thirty seconds are up, he should be calmer and more settled. If he's in his crate, now is the time to open the crate door and say calmly, "Okay." Tell him, still calmly, what a great dog he is and how pleased you are to see him. Ask him, "Do you need to go OUT?" and take him directly outside to the bathroom.

 Modeling calm, controlled behavior helps your dog to be calm and controlled, too.

Chapter 15

The Sociable Dog

Your dog's attitude toward people

Word #43: "People"

In one sense, "people" is simply an object word, like "biscuit"—so you can teach it like any other object word. When your dog sees or meets a person, you say, "People! See the PEOPLE? Look, people are coming! Good people!"

But in another sense, "people" is different from "biscuit" because most dogs have good feelings about biscuits, while individual dogs react very differently to people.

- Some dogs love everybody. My dog Buffy, as the saying goes, never met a stranger—she treats everyone she meets like a long-lost friend.
- Some dogs are fine with their own family and perhaps a few family friends, but aren't keen on strangers.
- Some dogs are fine with people of one sex, but not the other sex. "Tippy's fine with women," an owner will explain. "But he's afraid of men."
- Some dogs are fine with adults, but leery of children. (A few dogs are the opposite—they're fond of kids, but wary or suspicious of grown-ups.)

- Some dogs are suspicious of certain physical features—a beard, a hat, dark sunglasses. Some dogs react aggressively to uniforms (police officers, mail carriers, UPS drivers). A few dogs are so observant they notice skin color, and if it's different than what they're used to, they may react with suspicion.
- Some dogs dislike ALL strangers.
- And some dogs ignore people. They will glance at a stranger, then go back to sleep. Their motto is: "Live and let live."

Your dog's attitude toward other dogs

Word #44: "Doggy"

When I'm speaking to my dog about herself, I call her a *dog*. "Buffy, what a good DOG you are!"

But when I'm speaking to her about OTHER dogs, I call them *doggies*. "See that DOGGY? He's a good doggy!"

Just as individual dogs react very differently to people, they react very differently to other dogs.

- Some dogs are happy to meet other dogs.
- Some dogs are fine with other dogs they know well, but not so much with strange dogs.
- Some dogs are fine only with dogs of the opposite sex.
- Some dogs are extremely tolerant with puppies, but not with other adult dogs.
- Some dogs are fussy about the SIZE of another dog. Whatever their own size, they may dislike very large dogs or very small dogs.
- Some dogs are fussy about the BREED of the other dog. They may be fine with their own breed, but dislike other breeds.

(This is especially common in toy breeds, Dachshunds, and sighthounds.) Conversely, they may be fine with other breeds, but less so with their own breed. (This is common in fighting breeds like Pit Bull Terriers.)

- Some dogs are aggressive (or shy) with virtually every other dog.
- And some dogs just ignore other dogs. "Just leave me be and we'll get along fine," is their motto.

Why your dog is (or isn't) sociable

Your dog's attitude toward people and other dogs is partly the result of ...

his breed.

Some breeds inherit genes that make them suspicious toward strangers or dominant/aggressive toward other animals. Research your dog's breed for clues about the genes he may have inherited. Guarding breeds, mastiff breeds, livestock guardians, and terriers are likely to have inherited such genes because those traits helped them accomplish their intended work.

 It's much more difficult to change behavior that is genetically "hardwired" into a breed.

Your dog's attitude toward people and other dogs is partly the result of

his parents.

If your puppy's parents and grandparents were good-natured toward people and other dogs, there's a good chance they passed along those genes to their puppies. But if a parent or grandparent was aggressive or shy, they may have passed along those genes instead.

Your dog's attitude toward people and other dogs is partly the result of

how long he lived with his mother and siblings.

THE FIRST SEVEN WEEKS of a puppy's life are critical in determining how he will later act toward people and other dogs. This is because a puppy's mother and siblings teach him something called **bite inhibition**.

Bite inhibition means jaw control. If a puppy bites too hard during play, his mother or sibling will react dramatically, pouncing on the offending puppy and giving him a good shake or retaliatory bite. If the puppy responds properly to this chastisement, by becoming submissive, cringing abjectly, and pretty much shouting, "I'm sorry!" mother or sibling will be satisfied that they have gotten their message across.

In this way, a puppy learns to restrain his biting, to respect other dogs, and to recognize and respond properly to the social signals of dominance and submission.

A puppy removed from his mother and siblings before seven weeks of age missed these vital early lessons—so he frequently ends up being mouthy and nippy, resistant to being handled or corrected, or aggressive toward other dogs.

Now for the flip side…

A puppy shouldn't be left with his mother and siblings longer than twelve weeks. Why? Because by then, a pack order (pecking order) will have developed, and if a puppy is at the top of this ladder for too long, he may always be too dominant or aggressive toward people or other dogs. Conversely, if a puppy is at the bottom of the ladder for too long, he may always be on the submissive or timid side.

The moral? Bring home your puppy at seven to twelve weeks old. Or if you're considering a puppy older than twelve weeks, make sure the breeder separated the puppies prior to twelve weeks so each puppy could develop its own personality.

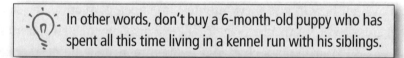

In other words, don't buy a 6-month-old puppy who has spent all this time living in a kennel run with his siblings.

Your dog's attitude toward people and other dogs is partly the result of

his early environment.

If your puppy was harmed or frightened by a person or another dog when he was young, he may end up aggressive or fearful. Early imprinting can be difficult to change.

Your dog's attitude toward people and other dogs is partly the result of

how he is handled during adolescence.

Adolescence starts at 6–9 months old and ends at 12–24 months old. Smaller dogs have the shorter adolescent periods, while larger dogs have the longer.

Adolescence in dogs (as in people) is an awkward time of change and upheaval. During adolescence, a dog's attitude toward the world may change from week to week—even from day to day! This is also a difficult time for owners, because up until then their puppy may have been getting along famously with the world. But during adolescence, when the hormones kick in, that sweet puppy may change—a lot. He may suddenly become skittish, spooky, or suspicious, especially between eight and eighteen months of age.

It may be temporary, just a stage that will pass in a few months...

IF the puppy came from good-natured parents, lived with his mother and siblings for seven to twelve weeks, and has always had positive experiences with strangers and other dogs. Just keep socializing him (I'll explain how in just a few minutes) and keep correcting any signs of aggression or skittishness (again, I'll explain how in a few minutes).

OR ... your puppy's changing temperament may be permanent as his genes or early environment begin to catch up with him. Unfortunately...

- if you chose a breed with a reputation for aggression...
- or if one of your puppy's parents had a poor temperament and passed those genes along to your puppy...
- or if your puppy was removed from his mother and siblings before seven weeks old so that he didn't receive bite inhibition training...

It may be too late to fix things. You can't change the genes your dog inherited and you can't go back in time and add positive experiences or undo negative experiences during the critical early weeks of his life.

> All you can do is to keep socializing and keep correcting signs of aggression or skittishness. It may make a difference—or it may not. Unfortunately, some temperament problems can't be fixed.

How to socialize your dog

Dogs feel most secure when they know how to interact positively with strangers and other dogs, and when they're comfortable with the sights and sounds of the big wide world.

Take your dog out into the world—don't keep him sheltered at home

Take him to:

- parks
- ball games
- playgrounds
- walking paths
- pet supply stores

Point out other people and dogs

"Look, Jake. A doggy. A GOOD doggy!"
"Look, Jake. People! GOOD people."

Associate strangers and other dogs with treats and play

When other people and dogs are around, become all smiles and laughter. Pull a toy from your pocket and play with your dog. Speak cheerfully to him, "Here's your TOY! What a GOOD dog you are! Yay!"

If his tail is up and wagging, give him treats and keep praising.

> If you sit in a crowd of people and reward your dog with food and play, he will be more likely to associate people with good things!

By the way, you can do exactly the same thing to accustom your dog to thunderstorms, gunshots, low-flying planes, fireworks, and emergency sirens. When the thunder starts rumbling, put on cheerful music, break out the toys and treats, and play with your dog. Encourage him to bounce around and give him treats when his tail comes up.

Professional trainers do this when they raise puppies to be guide dogs for the blind, or police dogs, or hunting dogs. It would be bad if these dogs were frightened by thunderstorms or sirens! So right from the get-go, savvy trainers turn Thunderstorm Time into Happy Time.

Interact with strangers and other dogs

Say "Hello" to lots of people. Ask them what time it is. Comment on the weather. If you see a dog who looks friendly, stop to pet it. Smile. Your dog can hear a smile in your voice, and he recognizes cheerfulness. You want to send him a message that you're happy to see other people and dogs.

> Your dog draws conclusions from YOUR mood. If you're happy and confident, he will conclude that the world is nothing to worry about. If you're tense and anxious, he is more likely to be, too.

Loosen your dog's leash

One of the most common mistakes owners make is holding their dog on a taut leash when they approach people and other dogs.

A taut leash makes some dogs more aggressive! They can literally feel your presence at the other end of the leash and they conclude that it's safe to threaten another dog or person because you're right there to "back them up." In other words, the leash becomes their umbilical cord. When they feel that connection, they act like Attila the Hun.

Conversely, a taut leash makes some dogs more timid or nervous because they feel trapped and unable to escape.

Finally, a taut leash communicates to your dog that you're concerned or worried about the situation, which makes HIM concerned and worried about the situation.

So don't hold your dog tightly beside you like this.

Instead, use the Quick Tug and Relax technique (Chapter 13) to keep the leash loose.

Letting strangers interact with your dog

Keep treats in your pocket. If anyone shows interest in your dog, tell them you're working on socializing him with people. Most people are happy to help with this. Hand them a treat and ask them to give it to your dog.

If they want to pet your dog and he's very small, ask them to turn their hand so their palm is facing UP and scratch their fingers against his throat and chest rather than patting his head. Demonstrate this with your own hand.

Many toy dogs hate hands descending from the sky onto their tiny heads! If too many people try to pet them like this, they may become hand-shy.

Letting other dogs interact with your dog

Be cautious about letting your dog sniff noses with other dogs. Personally, I prefer to know the other dog before I allow this. This is especially true when I'm socializing a puppy or a timid dog, where any mistake could have catastrophic consequences in his future attitude toward other dogs.

I'm even more cautious with toy dogs, so much so that I seldom allow a toy dog to sniff noses if the other dog is considerably larger. In fact, if a strange dog is bearing down on us, even if he is on a leash, I veer well away so that my toy dog is out of reach—or I pick up the toy dog, just for safety.

Don't underestimate the danger here. I have been the unhappy eyewitness to the horrifying spectacle of a large dog suddenly grabbing, shaking, and seriously injuring (and in one tragic case, actually killing) the smaller one. The speed with which it happens is unbelievable.

The problem is that larger dogs often view toy dogs as prey. A sudden movement, such as your toy dog pouncing on a leaf, can trigger chasing instincts even in a nice dog who means well. He can seize your little one before he even thinks about what he is doing—before you have time to move or draw a breath. It has happened time and time again.

Even if an owner assures you that his dog is good with other dogs

Take it with a grain of salt. Dog owners are always assuring people of their dog's friendliness and good nature. Just ask any (bitten) vet, groomer, or mail carrier how many times he or she has been told, "My dog would never bite."

Sad to say, many owners know little or nothing about their own dog. Even worse, they have little or no control over its behavior. This is especially a problem when two dogs are different sizes. Owners of larger dogs are often blissfully unaware that even a friendly head butt, or playful pawing, can harm a smaller dog.

For safety's sake, if you own a small dog, assume that:

- Other owners don't understand the prey instinct.
- The efforts of other owners to control and restrain their dog will be slow, weak, and ineffective.

How to correct aggressiveness or fearfulness

If your dog doesn't want to interact with other people or dogs, don't force him.

Some dogs, like some people, are introverts. If your dog hangs back a bit and isn't interested in interacting with people or other dogs, don't force the issue.

But don't accept

- barking
- growling
- woofing
- raised hackles
- lifted lip
- hiding behind your legs, tail tucked
- standing up on hind legs, pawing at you to be picked up
- bolting fearfully to the end of the leash, trying to escape
- lunging toward people or other dogs in an aggressive manner

If your dog displays any of those negative behaviors

1. Tell him firmly that such behaviors are unacceptable. "No. Stop that."
2. Use the Quick Tug and Release technique (Chapter 13) to maneuver your dog into a loose-leash position beside you.
3. Some dogs who are acting up benefit from being put into a Sit-Stay. A dog who is concentrating on something positive and specific, such as holding a Sit-Stay position, can't be doing something negative, such as trying to fight or run away.
4. You might even run him through a quick obedience routine, working on whatever words he knows so far: "Sit. Stand. Sit. Down. Stay. Come. Sit. Good boy!" Use your voice and the leash to keep his attention focused on YOU.

Don't "reassure" a dog who is displaying negative behaviors

Saying soothing things like "It's okay, it's all right, don't worry, nobody's going to hurt you" may seem like a perfectly natural thing to do—BUT your dog interprets petting and soothing words:

- as **praise** of his aggressive or fearful behavior
- or as **confirmation** that there is something to be concerned about but that YOU'LL protect him from it.

**You don't want to send EITHER
of those messages to your dog.**

Just focus on STOPPING the unacceptable behavior—by correcting it as you would any other unacceptable behavior. Tell your dog, "No" or "Stop that" and back it up with a physical correction, if necessary.

> Your dog doesn't have to LIKE people or other dogs. But he must ACCEPT them. He cannot express his negative FEELINGS through inappropriate BEHAVIOR.

Whatever corrections you have to make, once your dog is behaving appropriately, say goodbye to the other person or dog and stroll away. Tell your dog what a good boy he was and give him a treat. Even if he never becomes friendly and outgoing with people, he may actually come to look forward to meeting them—because he gets praise and a treat.

Please take this chapter seriously. Socialize your dog thoroughly and don't allow any display of aggressive behavior. Consider the legal and financial liabilities if you end up in civil or criminal court.

Fearfulness is just as dangerous as aggression

A dog who is afraid may react defensively by lashing out at anything that startles him. So don't think that just because you have a shy or timid dog, you don't have to worry about him biting anyone. Shyness can be a serious problem in dogs, especially in large breeds who can do

a lot of damage if they snap or bite—whether out of aggressiveness or out of anxiety or fear.

If you have a truly fearful dog

A book called **Help for Your Shy Dog** (by Deborah Wood) discusses all the problems that come with owning a shy dog, including submissive urination and fear-aggression. Many owners unknowingly "enable" their dog to be fearful, similar to the well-meaning family of an alcoholic, which covers for the dysfunctional person, and in so doing, supports the wrong habits.

Remember, DON'T do these three things with a fearful or suspicious dog:

1. Don't reassure him by telling him "It's okay."
2. Don't pick him up "to make him feel safe."
3. Don't tighten his leash to keep him close to you.

All of these reactions seem like perfectly natural responses to your dog's anxiety, but they actually encourage him to be even more nervous or suspicious.

Your dog's attitude toward children

There are three common myths about dogs and children:

(1) All dogs love children. (2) Dogs and children go together. (3) A dog would never harm a child.

Whereas the reality is that many dogs really don't like the loud voices, quick movements, and yo-yo emotions that are the natural characteristics of wee human beings.

- Sensitive dogs (such as toy dogs and sighthounds) are often startled by the unpredictability of children.

- Feisty dogs, such as terriers, often won't put up with nonsense from little life forms whom they view as below themselves in importance.

You can do everything right with your dog—train him well, socialize him well—and still, because of his genes, or his individual personality, or the arrangement of stars and planets in his horoscope, he may not like children.

**What he DOES have to do
is ACCEPT children.**

There's no mystery or special techniques in accomplishing that. Take your dog to parks, playgrounds, and ball fields, point out children ("People! Good people!"), praise good behavior, and correct unacceptable behavior.

Word #45: "Baby"

Because they're so vulnerable, I like to give infants and toddlers special status with a word of their own. I combine their special word with two other words my dog already knows: "Don't touch" and "Easy." Putting these words together, I present the infant or toddler to my dog as a **possession** of mine—and as such, something to be respected and unharmed.

"BABY. Easy. Don't touch. MINE."

Your dog's attitude toward cats

Word #46: "Cat" (or "Kitty Cat")

Some dogs sniff at felines in a friendly manner and may even attempt to play. If the cat is willing, their play usually takes the form of mild wrestling and mock chase games—where the cat often does as much chasing as the dog!

Some dogs ignore cats. They will glance at a cat, then go about their own business.

Some dogs are cautious around cats. It may be an instinctive caution, where the dog can tell from the cat's attitude or body language that there is something unusual about these small creatures that he had better respect.

Or it may be a learned caution, where he has actually encountered feline claws and discovered to his chagrin that cats should be avoided!

Some dogs are fine with cats in their own family, but not with strange cats.

 Some dogs will chase every cat they see but usually just for the fun of the pursuit. If the cat suddenly turns to defend itself, most dogs slam on the brakes and back off.

Finally, there are serious cat killers. These dogs will readily grab and kill a cat and may even deliberately stalk them.

Your dog's attitude toward cats is partly the result of

his breed.

Some breeds have a **high prey drive**, which means they see other creatures, especially smaller ones that flutter or run, as potential prey. This includes cats, small dogs, squirrels, hamsters, birds, rabbits, etc.

Dogs with a high prey drive have strong instincts to hunt or chase small critters, grab them, shake them, and/or kill them. Remember—most purebred dogs were developed as working dogs. They hunted, chased, stalked, guarded, and fought. So it really isn't surprising that many purebreds have a high prey drive.

Your dog's attitude toward cats is partly the result of

his first experiences with cats.

If a puppy was introduced to a carefully-chosen cat who held her ground and showed warning claws when the puppy got too pushy, there's a good chance he will develop the proper respect for cats.

If, on the other hand, the first cat he saw fled up a tree, his prey drive will be reinforced and he may become bolder and more aggressive toward small creatures that run.

Finally, if a big ol' tom cat turned on him and let him have both barrels, a puppy can be seriously hurt, not only physically, but also psychologically. He may end up terrified of cats—or obsessed with killing them.

> The moral? Introduce your dog to cats when he is a puppy. Try to find a friend with a dog-wise cat who knows how to put dogs in their place without hurting them.

Your dog's attitude toward cats is partly the result of

how you encourage him to react to cats.

If you're like me, you're annoyed at irresponsible cat owners who allow their cats to roam free—to use your garden as a litter box, to spray their urine against the wheels of your car, to get into your trash, to stalk the goldfish in your garden pond, and to ambush the wild birds who visit your feeders.

So why shouldn't your dog protect your property by chasing trespassing cats?

Concern #1: Your dog could injure or kill the cat.

A loose cat who damages your yard is a nuisance, yes, but the real problem is the owner who allows him to do so. No cat deserves to be hurt or terrified. You may also end up paying vet bills and the cat owner may retaliate by opening your gate or seeing that some other "accident" befalls your dog when you're not home.

Concern #2: Your dog won't be welcome in homes that have a cat.

If you have friends or relatives with cats, it will be difficult to take your cat-chasing dog with you when you visit.

Concern #3: Your dog could end up hit by a car.

Dogs who become enthusiastic cat chasers will dash through open doors, leap from car windows, climb over fences, and rush heedlessly across the street. Since you never know when a cat may appear from the shadows, cat-chasing dogs are risky to take anywhere.

Concern #4: The chased cat could fight back.

Feline teeth and claws carry lots of bacteria, which means cat scratches and bites are likely to become infected. And a dog who is hurt by a cat may develop psychological fears and neurotic behaviors.

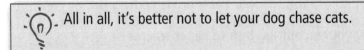
All in all, it's better not to let your dog chase cats.

How to handle cat chasing

Use cautionary words that your dog already knows:

"GOOD kitty. Easy! Don't touch! EASY with the kitty."

Make it clear to your dog, by your strong tone of voice (and leash corrections if necessary) that you are claiming the cat as YOUR possession—and as such, it must be respected and unharmed.

If your dog persists in barking or pestering, "No! Leave it" may jolt him away from his focus. A squirt gun or spray bottle (sometimes a hose for large dogs) is often effective in discouraging your dog from pestering a cat.

Your dog's attitude toward other critters

Word #47: "Squirrel"

What about squirrels? Should you encourage your dog to chase squirrels?

Again there is the **pro** side—it seems like a good idea to send your dog after squirrels who dig holes in your garden, bury nuts in your flowerpots, and monopolize your bird feeders. And most dogs love chasing squirrels.

But again there is the **con** side—squirrel-driven dogs who forget boundary training and self-control in their lust to get the squirrel. They dash through open doors, slip their collars, jump out of your car, and so on.

> Dogs who have been encouraged to chase things often do so at the worst possible time. And then they never chase anything again.

Also consider the fear and panic of the fleeing squirrel. Even if you know that your particular dog has virtually no chance of catching or harming the squirrel, do you really want to be entertained by an exciting chase if the cost is a terrified little creature?

Finally, consider that some dogs who start with chasing squirrels progress to chasing other creatures—such as your neighbor's cat or small dog. And what if you decide to bring home a guinea pig for your kids?

If you decide to prohibit your dog from chasing squirrels, you can still teach him the word. "See the SQUIRREL? Good squirrel. Easy. Don't touch."

Words #48–50: Other Animals

Songbirds may frequent your feeders, or you may have a parakeet or canary. Wild rabbits may hop through your yard, or your kids may have a Holland Lop or New Zealand White. You may have a pet ferret. You may own a horse, or horses may live across the road. You may keep chickens or goats. Deer may graze nearby. Skunks or raccoons may wander through your back yard at dusk.

Expand your dog's vocabulary by teaching him the names of these animals:

"Ferret. GOOD ferret. Easy! Don't touch! EASY with the FERRET."

 It's a nice feeling when your dog is peaceful toward other living creatures.

Chapter 16
The Playful Dog

The best toys for your dog

For exercising jaws and mind, relieving boredom, and venting energy, I recommend these toys:

Nylabones®. In my opinion, these are the safest commercial chew toys. But even Nylabones require very careful monitoring. I never allow my dog to EAT one of these hard nylon chews, but only to gnaw on the ends until they're frayed. Then I throw it out and buy a new one.

Kong® toys. Made of thick, heavy rubber and often enjoyed by vigorous dogs with strong jaws.

Cotton Rope Toys and Nylafloss®. These massage and floss your dog's teeth and gums. Take them away when they get frayed. (If your dog pulls out individual strings and swallows them, these toys are not safe for him.)

Balls. Many dogs love the fuzziness of tennis balls. Hard rubber balls may also be appreciated, though these balls can sting if you accidentally hit your dog when you throw one. Small dogs often prefer soft rubber balls, especially hollow ones that squish so they're easily gripped by small mouths.

> ⟨💡⟩ Be careful with the size of the ball! Make absolutely sure your dog can't swallow it. If he is a chewer, soft rubber isn't safe and neither is a squeaker inside.

Stuffed (plush) toys. IF your dog doesn't destroy them. Remove plastic eyes and nose, ribbons, bowties, stringy tails, care labels, etc. Avoid beanbag toys—guess why?

Homemade toys include old socks or towels knotted together, and plastic water jugs or mouthwash bottles with the cap removed. Again, these toys are only suitable for dogs who are not serious chewers. For interactive fun, tie a string or rope to these toys and drag them around for your dog to chase.

Always think safety! Replace socks when they fray. Replace plastic jugs when they get punctured enough to have sharp edges.

The worst toys for your dog

Rawhide. Can peel off in soggy strips and choke your dog, or obstruct his stomach or intestines. Often processed with chemicals such as lye.

Pig's ears. Become soggy and slippery and can lodge in your dog's throat. Ingredients-wise, they are loaded with fat and can cause diarrhea and vomiting. To top it off, they stink and can stain your carpet.

Cow's hooves. Can break into sharp slivers that can punch through your dog's throat and intestines.

So-called "ingestible" chews such as cornstarch bones and Greenies®. Despite the marketing hype, dogs were never intended to eat the ingredients in these things and dogs have choked to death on them.

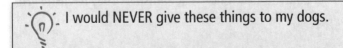

> ⟨💡⟩ I would NEVER give these things to my dogs.

Anything that says *smoked.* Loaded with cancer-linked nitrites and preservatives.

Soft rubber/vinyl toys. Lightweight squeaky toys are fine for very gentle, non-chewing dogs (especially small dogs) who like to carry them around, chase and retrieve them, even sleep with them. But many dogs destroy them in about thirty seconds and some dogs swallow the pieces, including squeakers or bells inside.

> Know your own dog! Never assume that just because a toy is offered for sale at the pet store that it must be safe for your particular dog.

How many toys in the Toy Box?

If your dog does not have any rude behaviors

Provide many toys of different sizes, shapes, and textures. Toys stimulate your dog's mind as he pokes, prods, mouths, and figures out how to play with the toy. Offer a variety of Nylabones®, hard rubber toys, balls, ropes, knotted socks—and for SOME dogs, carefully-chosen stuffed animals, soft rubber, or vinyl toys that squeak or make other interesting noises.

I recommend **rotating** toys to maintain your dog's interest. Let him have a few toys for two or three weeks, then put them away and offer a different set of toys.

Rotating toys keeps your dog's mind open to accepting new things, which is a healthy attitude. You don't want a rigid dog who is so focused on one special toy that he gets upset when it can't immediately be located. Removing familiar toys for a few weeks also makes them seem new and exciting when you return them.

However, if your dog has any rude behaviors or if he is a destructive chewer

Pick up all toys except for two.

Giving lots of stuff to a spoiled dog is as unwise as giving lots of stuff to a spoiled child. Pick up the toys until your dog's behavior improves.

If he is a destructive chewer, it's especially important to pick up most toys. Because if the floor is littered with a zillion toys, your dog may assume that **everything** is a toy and is potentially chewable, including your belongings.

With a destructive chewer, I do not rotate toys, but instead choose two toys, and two toys only. This makes it more clear to him that these two objects are the only things he is allowed to chew on. Everything else receives a "No" or "Don't touch" and is off limits.

The good news is that most destructive chewers grow out of the habit with maturity, increased exercise, and respect training. So it won't be too long before you'll be able to add more toys to your dog's Toy Box and begin rotating them for variety.

Dealing with possessiveness

If your dog ever becomes overly possessive of a toy and won't give it to you, or growls over it when you approach him, take it away immediately.

For a full month.

In this way, he may come to appreciate that toys are not free gifts, but are privileges that you can bestow and take away, based on his behavior.

To **avoid** possessiveness, work on the next exercise.

"Give"–teach your dog to let go of his toys

Word #51: "Give"

There will be many times in your dog's life when you want him to give up an object that he is clutching in his mouth.

"Jake, let go!" Kathy said in frustration. Her dog had pounced on her scarf and was now clinging to it while Kathy tugged fruitlessly at the other end. R-i-i-i-p-p! went the scarf, and Kathy wailed in despair, let go of her end, and grabbed Jake's head before he could escape with his prize. With both hands, she tried to pry his jaws apart. Jake wagged his tail good-naturedly, but refused to let go.

How frustrating! The solution is to teach your dog to relinquish any object—including his toys—when you tell him to.

Here's how to teach "Give"

1. Play with your dog—get him romping around with a toy or stick or sock in his mouth.
2. When he cavorts close enough to you that you can take hold of his collar without needing to snatch at him, do so. A grip on his collar gives you control of his head.
3. In a cheerful voice, say "Jake, give!" and try to take the toy from his mouth. If he lets go, praise him and give the toy right back to him so he can play with it some more.

    In real life, you will often take things away from him that he can't have back. But when you're teaching this word, he will be much more willing to go along with it if he gets the object back!
4. If he **didn't** give up the toy, you'll need to open his mouth and take it.

There are two ways to get your dog to open his mouth:

- Pressure on his **lower** jaw. Place your hand under his jaw, palm up. Your thumb should be on one side of his jaw, your four fingers on the other side. Using all five fingers, press his LIPS firmly inward against his TEETH as you say again, "Give!" If you're pressing in the right place, his mouth will open. Take the toy and praise him!
- Pressure on his **upper** jaw. Place your hand on TOP of his muzzle. Your thumb should be on one side of his muzzle, your four fingers on the other side, with the top of his muzzle nestled in the fleshy crook of your hand between your thumb and forefinger. Press all five fingers against his lips so that his lips press inward against his teeth. His mouth should open.

    As soon as you have the toy, praise him with enthusiasm, just as you would if he had given it up of his own accord. Toss it for him again so he can play with it again.

5. Practice with a variety of items—most of which you should return to him. As a change of pace, take an object from him and give him a treat in return.

> Soon he should be willing to give up whatever he has in his mouth, knowing you will probably give it back to him or will substitute a tasty treat.

"Drop" (whatever is in his mouth)

Word #52: "Drop"

If your dog picks up something he shouldn't, you need a word that tells him to open his mouth and DROP it onto the ground.

You're thinking, "Wait a minute! I just taught my dog to "Give!" Yes, that does work for many objects. But do you really want your dog to spit a half-chewed cigarette butt or dead bug into your hand?

No, it's better to use "Give" when you want your dog to actually relinquish something into your **hand**.

When you simply want him to spit something out, even when you're some distance away from him, a better word is "Drop."

Here's how to teach "Drop"

1. Play with your dog—get him romping around with a toy or stick or sock in his mouth.
2. Suddenly call out, "Jake, DROP!" Your tone of voice is important—it should be firm and commanding, but not angry.
3. If he actually drops the toy (often from sheer surprise), praise him. Quickly pick up the toy and toss it for him so he can have it again.

   In real life, you usually need him to drop things that he can't have back. But when you're teaching this word, he will be much more willing to go along with it if he discovers that he will get the object back.
4. If he didn't drop the toy, that's not a problem. He hasn't yet learned this yet, after all. Walk toward him, keeping your body language relaxed and smiling. Don't stalk toward him as though he's done something wrong! In a calm, friendly manner, take

hold of his collar. Say again, "Drop!" and gently open his mouth (you learned how to do that with "Give") so the toy falls to the ground. Praise him, pick up the toy, and toss it for him.

5. As when you were teaching "Give," practice "Drop" with a variety of items—most of which you should return to him. As a change of pace, have him drop an object and give him a treat in return.

Tug-of-war games

Word #53: "Tug"

If your dog has a strong-willed, dominant, really feisty, or aggressive personality, or if he is displaying rude behaviors (hopefully you're working on these!)...

Tug-of-war is one of the WORST possible games.

Do you really want to encourage such a dog to clamp down with his teeth, growl, shake his head, resist and fight against you? Not hardly!

 "What about if my dog is sweet and gentle and doesn't have any rude behaviors?"

Then tug-of-war can be great fun for both of you—as long as YOU always win the game.

Here's how to play tug-of-war with a sweet, gentle, well-behaved dog

1. When your dog brings you a suitable tug toy (rope, knotted sock, floppy stuffed animal) and tries to get you to play with him, take hold of one end and encourage him, in a cheerful

voice, to "Tug! Tug!" Play for only about ten or twenty seconds, then stop tugging, hold your hand very still on your end of the toy, and say, "That's ENOUGH. GIVE!"

2. Your dog knows both these words and should let go of the toy. Praise him, offer the toy again and resume the game for another ten or twenty seconds, then end it again with "Enough. Give." Give him lots of praise, give him the toy back to do with as he chooses, and go about your own business.

On the off chance that your dog didn't let go of the toy when you told him to, you know how to open his mouth and take the toy away (Word #51: Give). If you actually have to do this, you need to spend some more time working on "Give" before you play any more tug games with him.

> ☀ Never let your dog run away with the toy! Tug is a game that he should not win. He will have plenty of fun PLAYING the game—he doesn't need to win. The psychological aspects of winning this contest are so important that you should reserve them for yourself.

If your dog becomes overexcited during this game, vigorously trying to tear the toy away from you, fiercely growling or snarling, or grabbing at your hand instead of the tug toy...

Say sharply, "Ah-ah! No! Stop that!" Stop the play and have him "Give" you the toy. Hold the toy in front of him and warn him, "Easy! Easy!" If his body language appears chastised and repentant, resume the play, but make it a much less vigorous game. Remain watchful. A repeated offense of over excitement or aggression warrants an immediate end to the game. And don't let him have the toy—put it away.

Many dogs simply can't play any kind of tug game because it makes them more dominating and disrespectful.

Young children should not play tug of war with a dog. Children can't judge when a dog is out of control and they can't correct a dog with enough authority when his behavior goes over the line.

Teach your dog to "fetch" a toy

Word #54: "Toy"

In the beginning, you may want to call ALL of your dog's toys, simply, **TOY**. Later we'll give individual names to some of them—and we'll teach your dog to differentiate between them.

But in the beginning, especially when your dog is just a puppy, it will be easier for him to learn the concept that ALL of his playthings have the same appellation: **TOY**.

"TOY!"

Teaching this concept is simple. Each time you play with him, show him the toy and name it. "TOY! See the TOY? Good TOY!"

Remember to emphasize the word you want him to learn. A few extra words are okay, but too many will dilute the importance of the one word you want him to pick out.

Shake the toy, bounce it, roll it, toss it, do whatever it takes to get your dog looking at the toy, and over time, recognizing that his playthings have a specific sound.

Word #55: "Fetch" (or "Get It")

Once your dog knows the word toy, you'd probably like him to **do** something with the toy. To run after it when you throw it. To bring it back so you can throw it again.

We call this **retrieving**, or more informally, **fetching**.

The good news is that some dogs are natural retrievers.

The bad news is that most dogs are not!

Some dogs are natural retrievers

Sporting (gundog) breeds, such as spaniels, setters, and retrievers, are often natural retrievers because they were developed to find and **fetch** game birds for hunters.

Herding breeds, such as collies and shepherds, are often natural retrievers. They were developed to **chase and gather moving sheep** so it's usually easy to extend those chasing and gathering instincts to thrown objects.

And some small breeds, such as Poodles, Papillons, Jack Russell Terriers, Fox Terriers, and Boston Terriers, are often natural retrievers.

But most dogs are NOT natural retrievers

Breeds such as Beagles and Basset Hounds are examples of hunting dogs who DON'T have retrieving instincts. They track down prey, sometimes kill it, but they don't bring it back to the hunter. Thus, they have strong chasing instincts and might run after something you throw for them, but they will seldom bring it back.

The same is true of "northern" breeds such as Alaskan Malamutes, Siberian Huskies, and Akitas. They have strong predatory (chasing) instincts, but they're more inclined to eat their prey—not bring it back.

Similarly, terriers were developed to chase and kill vermin, not fetch it to you. Most terriers are too possessive and independent to bring things to people. They would rather keep things to themselves! (Although some small terriers, especially Fox Terriers and Jack Russells, do seem to be "hardwired" with retrieving instincts. In fact, they're often obsessive retrievers!)

"If my dog is not a natural retriever, are fetch games hopeless?"

Not necessarily. A dog who is not a natural retriever may still be able to learn to retrieve. But the training process can be difficult because you're going against your breed's natural instincts.

Here's an example of how difficult retrieving is for many dogs:

In AKC obedience competition, many dogs succeed at the novice level, but far fewer succeed at the intermediate and advanced levels. Why? Because at the novice level, dogs simply have to heel, sit, lie down, stand, stay, and come. Every dog can learn those things. But at the intermediate and advanced levels, dogs have to retrieve—and that single requirement knocks out a whole lotta dogs!

So if you have a dog who won't retrieve, don't feel alone. You can try to teach him, but don't get discouraged if the training doesn't go as quickly or smoothly as you'd like.

There are many ways to teach retrieving.

The Natural Retriever Method (puppies and adults)

Choose a long hallway in your house. Close all the doors along it, so that once your dog has run down the hallway he can't duck into any side rooms.

Get your dog excited about his toy. When he's barking and jumping for it, toss it down the hall. Encourage him, "Get your toy! Get it!" or "Fetch your toy! Fetch!"

If he runs to get it and, miracle of miracles, brings it back to you, tell him cheerfully, "Give" and take it from him—or just "Drop" so he drops it on the floor.

There! Wasn't that easy?

Of course, there are any number of things that can go wrong!

- If your dog brings the toy back to you, but hangs on and refuses to give it up, that's not a problem. You know how to open his mouth and make him "Give" it or "Drop" it. (Words #51 and 52).
- If he runs to the toy and picks it up, but won't come back with it, or if he grabs it and runs off with it, call him: "Jake, come!" If he obeys, praise him (if he happens to bring the toy along with him, that's an extra bonus!) But if he drops the toy along the way, that's okay, too—just go get it yourself, and try again.
- If he refuses to obey your "Come" command, forget about the fetch game and make sure he obeys "Come." (Word #31.) Remember, he must obey that essential word **every time**.

If you try the Natural Retriever Method repeatedly and your dog chases the toy but never brings it back—or if he won't chase the toy at all—you'll need to decide how important it is to you that your dog retrieve.

Because there ARE step-by-step methods that will teach most dogs to retrieve. But they're a bit complicated, so I prefer not to use these methods until a dog is an adult and able to pay close attention.

The Systematic Food Method (adult dogs)

If your dog is a chowhound who will do almost anything for a food reward, this method may work for him!

You will systematically teach your dog to

- take a toy from your hand
- hold the toy without dropping it
- reach for the toy when you hold it away from him
- bring the toy back to you when you toss it

This method works best when your dog is hungry, so skip his morning meal for a couple of weeks while you're teaching this exercise. Don't worry about him STAYING hungry. He'll be getting plenty of food during your practice sessions.

Choose a soft treat that's easy to gulp down. Tiny pieces of cheddar cheese (REAL cheese, not processed American cheese) or cooked chicken work well. Or small kibbles. Don't use a treat that takes too long to chew or that scatters on the floor and distracts your dog as he snuffles around for crumbs.

Choose a toy that fits comfortably in his mouth. It shouldn't be so small that it could roll back into his throat. And it shouldn't be so bulky that it would be uncomfortable. A wooden training dumbbell, available at pet supply stores, is a good choice for teaching retrieving.

First, teach your dog to open his mouth for the toy

1. With the treats in your pocket, choose an area that's quiet and free of distractions. Get your leashed dog sitting on your left side. Kneel down and tuck the leash under your knees so both your hands are free but you still have control of him.

2. With your left hand, hold onto his collar. With your right hand, hold the toy in front of his mouth so it is actually touching his mouth. In a cheerful voice, say, "Get it!" or "Fetch!" He probably won't open his mouth, so you'll have to help him, like so:

    Take your left hand off his collar and place it on TOP of his muzzle. Your thumb should be on the right side of his muzzle, your four fingers on the left side, with the top of his muzzle nestled in the fleshy crook of your hand between your thumb and forefinger. Got that so far? Now press all five fingers against his lips so that his lips press inward against his teeth. His mouth should open. With your right hand, quickly place and hold the toy in his mouth as you repeat, "Get it!"

3. After only a few seconds, praise him, "Good boy!" and say, "Give" as you remove the toy from his mouth. Immediately give him a treat.

4. Repeat the exercise four more times, then STOP. Later in the day, do another five repetitions.

   If this method is going to work for your dog, by the end of the week he should be voluntarily opening his mouth when you touch the toy against his lips.

Next, teach your dog to hold the toy

1. Place it in his mouth and say, "Hold it." Put one hand under his chin, stroking it a bit to keep his muzzle tilted slightly upward so he is less likely to spit out the toy. Praise him softly, "Go-oo-od boy" as he holds the toy.

2. After only a few seconds, say, "Give." Remove the toy, praise him, and give him a treat.

   If at any point he tries to spit out the toy, try to intercept him by saying, "Ah-ah" and quickly closing his muzzle around the toy. If he does manage to spit it out, simply start again. Replace it in his mouth and say, "Hold it."

3. Once he is holding the toy reliably, move your hand farther away from his mouth. Gradually increase the time he holds the toy to ten seconds. That's long enough.

Now teach him to move around with the toy in his mouth

1. When he will hold the toy for ten seconds without your hand on his mouth supporting it, give him the toy to hold.

2. After only a few seconds, suddenly stand up and say, "Come, Jake!" Quickly place one hand under his chin to help keep his head up and holding the toy. Hook your other hand in his collar under his neck and guide him to follow you as you walk backward a few steps.

As before, if he tries to spit out or drop the toy, try to intercept him by saying, "Ah-ah" and quickly closing his muzzle around the toy. If it does fall to the ground, simply start again by replacing it in his mouth and saying, "Hold it."

3. Work up to moving your hand completely away from his mouth as you walk backward. You want him to be able to follow you around holding the toy.

4. Since he knows how to "Sit" and "Stay" and "Come," you can also put him in a Sit-Stay, holding the toy, and have him Come to you, still holding the toy (hopefully!).

Finally, teach him to reach for the toy

1. Once your dog will hold the toy as you both walk around, you can progress to this final step. With your dog STANDING on your left side, hold onto his collar with your left hand. With your right hand, flash the toy an inch in front of his nose. Say, "Get it."

    If he reaches forward and takes it, remind him to "Hold it." If he holds it, praise him, "Good boy!" Say, "Give" and take it from him. Praise and treat! Good job!

    If he DIDN'T reach forward to take it, use your grip on his collar to move him toward the toy until his mouth presses against it and he does take it. Praise him! Say "Give" and take it from him. Treat!

2. Once he has this down pat, encourage him to reach farther for the toy. Offer it a couple of inches in front of his nose. "Get it." When he reaches toward it, turn smoothly clockwise as you sweep the toy slowly away from him at eye level. This encourages him to "chase" and grab it.

3. When he can catch the moving toy held a full arm's length away, begin lowering it toward the floor. Make sure he has to bend further down each time to catch it. Soon you will place

it on the floor just in front of you, with your fingers touching it, then with your hand near it but not touching it.

4. Finally, toss it in front of you only a couple of feet away. At first you may need to point to the toy and urge him to pick it up. You may need to step forward and touch the toy as you encourage him to come pick it up. But soon he should be moving forward to retrieve it on his own.

> And there you have it—a step-by-step program for teaching a food-oriented dog to retrieve. As with all retrieving methods, it works for some dogs, and not for others.

The Compulsive Method (adult dogs)

If your dog doesn't respond to the Systematic Food Method and you really do want him to learn to retrieve, consider the compulsive method.

Compulsive means that you make your dog retrieve. It sounds grim, but when you think about it, anything we require our dogs to do is "compulsive." When you tell your dog to "Come," you add positive consequences when he comes, and negative consequences when he doesn't. That's compulsive. One way or the other, he has to Come.

The Compulsive Retrieve works the same way.

You start out by teaching your dog to open his mouth and hold the toy, just as you did with the Systematic Food Method.

But when you get to the step where your dog must reach forward for the toy, you add a negative consequence if he refuses.

A negative consequence means pinching his ear between your thumb and forefinger until he reaches forward to take the toy.

Now, calm down! With your thumb and forefinger, right now, pinch your own earlobe. Don't use your finger NAILS—just the PADS of your fingers. It's annoying, but certainly not excruciating, right?

The Compulsive Method produces the most reliable retriever. Even if your dog is distracted by something, he will fetch whatever you send him after, because he knows there will be negative consequences if he doesn't.

If you'd like to try this method, I recommend a book called ***Beyond Basic Dog Training*** (by Diane Bauman). It covers the Compulsive Retrieve, plus other precision obedience exercises if you're interested in serious obedience competition.

Teach your dog to "bring" you a toy

Suppose your dog picks up a toy and you'd like him to bring it to you. Since he's already holding it in his mouth, it doesn't make sense to tell him to "Fetch it!", right?

You need a different phrase:

Word #56: "Bring It Here"

HOW you teach this word depends on the specific situation. At this point in your dog's training, you have several helpful words at your disposal that you can combine to guide your dog into the behavior you want him to do.

Let's look at an example:

Your dog picks up a toy and stands looking at you. Say, "BRING your toy! BRING it here!" Crouch down and clap your hands to encourage him to come to you.

If he doesn't come, or if he runs off with the toy, call him with "Come!" Yes, he might drop the toy as he runs toward you, but you can still praise him for obeying "Come" and then quickly send him back after the toy with "GET it! Get your toy!"

(Assuming he has already learned to retrieve, of course. With non-retrieving dogs, there simply isn't a way to get them to go pick up a dropped toy and bring it to you.)

If your retrieving dog does go back to pick up the toy and starts to head toward you with it, add the new phrase, "BRING it here!"

> You want him to connect the phrase "Bring it here!" with the action of heading toward you with something in his mouth.

"Bring it here" is also useful when your dog has picked up something that you want to take away.

For example, my dog Buffy is often delighted to discover my nightgown on the bed, and she runs off with it. This isn't a crime, but I would like to have my nightgown back! So I tell her, "Bring it here!" I praise her for bringing it to me. I tell her to "Give" and I "trade" the nightgown for one of her own toys—or a treat.

Teach your dog to "find" a toy

Word #57: "Find It"

"Where's your toy? Find your toy!" is learned eagerly by natural retrievers (or those who have learned to retrieve by one of the other methods described above).

Even for a dog who won't retrieve, "Find your toy!" can be a fun game. You may be able to coax him into searching for and locating his toy, even if he won't bring it back to you.

So let's give it a try:

1. Choose a favorite toy for your dog to find. (Pick up all of his other toys and put them away so he won't become confused.)
2. Place the chosen toy across the room so he can see it. Encourage him, "Where's your TOY? FIND your TOY!"
3. Some dogs will immediately run to the toy, but most will need help. Guide your dog toward the toy by pointing and motioning. Walk toward it, gently clapping your hands to encourage him to follow. If necessary, go right up to the toy and touch it—anything to help him succeed.
4. When he finally spots it, use the familiar words, "Get it! Get your toy!" or if he's already picked it up, "Bring it here! Bring your toy!"
5. Once he understands that "Find!" means he needs to scout around and use his eyes and nose to search for something, you can place his toy in another room and send him after it.

Be supportive and helpful. Don't just stand there and watch your dog fail! Follow him around and encourage him, "Where is it? Where's your toy? Find it! Good boy!"

**Never allow your dog to fail
when you tell him to "Find" something.**

If he can't find it, or if he becomes discouraged and stops looking, it's up to you to help him succeed, even if you have to lead him right to the toy. He will only develop confidence and persistence if you show him that the toy IS findable—every single time.

When there are multiple toys lying about, your dog should be allowed to choose whichever toy catches his eye or appeals to him at the moment. I enjoy watching my dog select which toy she wants to bring to me. I wonder what criteria she uses to decide—are dogs "in the mood" for certain toys at certain times? It's a mystery!

"Find your cookie!"

For dogs who have absolutely no interest in finding a toy, have them find treats instead.

Hide a treat under a crumpled towel and tell your dog, "Where's your cookie? Find it!" Show him how to sniff and snuffle under the towel looking for the treat.

The musical toys game

Place one of your dog's toys across the room. Beside it, place a very unappealing **non**-toy, such as a hammer or dictionary!

Send your dog to "Get your TOY!" (I hope it goes without saying that you should make sure he retrieves the toy, and not the hammer or dictionary!)

Repeat this with different toys until he can't help but get the idea that **TOY** means his own personal playthings—any of them.

Now we'll make the game a lot more challenging (and fun) by teaching him the names of individual toys.

Words #58–62: Individual Toys

Which toys are your dog's favorites? Ball? Rope? Sock? Bone? Certain stuffed animals? Name them!

Here's how I taught my dog Buffy the names of her stuffed rabbit, duck, teddy, and dolly.

 I put away all toys except the rabbit. For a few days she and I played only with the rabbit. She carried it around and wrestled with it and I used every opportunity to name it for her: "Is that RABBIT? Do you have RABBIT? Good RABBIT!"

I threw it for her, encouraging her to "Get RABBIT!" I hid it in another room, encouraging her to "Find RABBIT!" Of course, with no other toys to choose from, she brought the rabbit every time.

Then I brought out her stuffed duck. I placed them side by side and said, "Get RABBIT!" The first time I tried this, she grabbed the rabbit. Wow! She was a genius!

Well, not exactly. The second time I sent her for the rabbit, she tried to pick up the duck. But I was watching for this, and the instant she put her mouth around it, I said, "Ah-ah" and she shied away from it. "Get RABBIT!" I encouraged her cheerfully. She grabbed the rabbit. "Good girl!" I said.

During one attempt, she was too quick. She seized the duck and brought it to me. In a very mild voice, I said, "No-no" and put it back with the rabbit so she could try again. Soon she learned that she only got praise when she got the rabbit.

After a few days of fetching the rabbit, I put it away entirely and focused on the stuffed duck. "Is this your DUCK?" and "Get your DUCK!" and "Find your DUCK!" Then I put the duck beside another toy (NOT the rabbit yet) and she retrieved the duck while ignoring the unnamed toy.

The hard part came when I placed the rabbit and the duck side by side. I sent her first for one, then the other. Now she had to remember which word went with which toy!

 This game really develops your dog's thinking skills and memory.

Once your dog knows several toys by name, you can play Musical Toys! Gather all the toys whose names your dog has learned and place them in a small group on the floor.

Then send him after each one, one at a time:

"Get your rabbit!" "Good boy!" "Give!"

"Get your duck!" "Good boy!" "Give!"

"Get teddy!" "Good boy!" "Give!"

"Get dolly!" "Good girl!" "Give!"

I play a similar game with Buffy where I send her in search of a specific toy. For example, "Find DOLLY!" She runs from room to room, rejecting all other toys in favor of Dolly, which she eventually locates and brings to me. If she can't find Dolly on her own, I go with her on a Dolly Hunt until we find it together.

If at any time she returns with the wrong toy, I take it from her, saying gently, "No no... find DOLLY!" Then I go with her on a Dolly Hunt.

Remember, make sure your dog succeeds!

Teach your dog the names of family members

Words #63-66: Names Of Family Members

Your dog can learn the names of the people in your family. Many owners refer to each other as Mommy and Daddy. Grandparents are often referred to as Grandma and Grandpa. And of course there are the kids.

To teach people's names, simply refer to them by name whenever your dog sees them. "There's DADDY! See DADDY?"

Also refer to them by name when your dog is ABOUT to see them. For example, when Daddy is coming up the walk, alert your dog ("Here comes Daddy! Daddy's coming!"), and when Daddy actually opens the door, switch to "Here's Daddy! Daddy's home!"

Make sure Daddy is within seconds of opening the door before you alert your dog.

 When introducing new words, deliver on your promises quickly so your dog makes the connection!

Word #67: "Go To (Family Member)"

Fun game! Send your dog back and forth from one person to another.

1. Start with only two people. Each person crouches or kneels down, facing each other about fifteen feet apart.
2. One person holds the dog by his collar and says, in an excited voice, "GO to Mommy!" Whereupon Mommy calls, "Jake, come!"
3. When Jake runs to Mommy, he is greeted with praise and a treat. She takes hold of his collar, points him in Daddy's direction, and says, "GO to Daddy!"
4. Three times to each person is enough for one practice session.

Add other family member one at a time. Eventually everyone can form a circle and play round robin, sending your dog around the circle to various family members. Only the named family member may give him a treat.

The hide and seek game

This game needs no explanation except for how to teach it. Daddy is going to hide, although his first "hiding place" should be no hiding place at all. Daddy should simply stand across the room in plain sight.

"Where's Daddy? Find Daddy!" For a dog as bright as yours, this is a no-brainer! When your dog rushes over, Daddy rewards with praise and play.

Next, Daddy hides behind a door in the next room. "Where's Daddy? Find Daddy!" Some dogs will get the idea immediately and begin scouting around, sniffing the floor or air-scenting (trying to pick up Daddy's scent from the air). Did you know that we're constantly shedding dead skin cells? That's the "scent" a dog follows when he tracks someone.

Other dogs will need a lot of help with this game. Go with your dog as you motion with your hands to guide him toward possible hiding places. Peek behind doors and shower curtains, behind chairs and sofas. Make sure your dog looks, too. "Where's Daddy? Is Daddy here? Find him!"

But look for only a **minute or two** before you "stumble upon" Daddy's hiding place. Celebrate with whoops and cheers "Yay! It's Daddy! You found Daddy!"

> Eventually you can be more creative with your hiding places, but make sure your dog succeeds every time. Never let a search go on for more than a couple of minutes or your dog will become anxious, discouraged, or bored. If Lassie can't find Timmy within a minute or two, lead her directly to the well so she's successful!

Teach your dog the names of other pets

Words #68–69: Names of Family Pets

If you own other dogs or cats, there are three reasons your dog should learn the individual names of each pet.

1. When you need to correct one pet, using its name will reassure the others that they need not worry, that they're not the one in trouble! "Buffy. This is bad!"

2. When you're giving treats, using each pet's name as you offer the treat cautions the others to wait their turn.

   For example, with both Luke and Buffy sitting in front of you, focus your gaze on Luke. Say, "Luke" and offer him a treat. If Buffy tries to grab it, correct her. "Ah-ah! Buffy, no." Give Luke a reassuring pat on the head and try again. Buffy will soon get the message that "Luke" refers to the OTHER dog.

3. Finally, if your dog has learned "Find it," he may be able to search for a specifically-named pet. "Buffy, where's Luke? Find Luke!" could come in handy if Luke isn't responding to your calls.

 Now, realistically speaking, most likely Luke is simply snoring under the bedcovers and won't appreciate it when Buffy jumps on him! But YOU'LL be relieved to know where he is. And if Luke really was trapped somewhere, Buffy might be able to track him down.

Hey, it's possible!

Chapter 17

Advanced Words

Teach your dog to "GO" wherever you send him

Your dog has learned the word GO as part of several phrases:

- Go crate.
- Go outside.
- Go car.
- Go lie down.
- Go for a walk?
- Go home.
- Go to Daddy!

There are many more places your dog can "Go."

Word #70: "Go Stairs"

You'll get a real workout with this one! With your dog at your side and treats in your pocket, stand at the bottom of a staircase.

Point your arm dramatically up the stairs. Tell your dog, in an excited voice, "Go stairs!" and RUN upstairs with him. Give him a treat when you reach the top.

Now point dramatically down the stairs. Say, "Go stairs!" and RUN downstairs with him. Give him a treat at the bottom.

If you want, you can say "UPstairs" for going up. But don't say, "DOWNstairs" for going down. It's better to reserve "Down" for one meaning and one meaning only—to lie down. Lying down and going downstairs are two very different actions, so you're likely to confuse your dog if you use "Down" in any way other than to lie down.

When my dog Buffy is lying on the sofa, I pretend to sneak toward the stairs. She raises her head, watching me intently. Her muscles tense. Suddenly I shout, "I'm going UPstairs!" and I make a mad dash for the stairs. She leaps off the sofa, barking happily, and chases me up the stairs.

Retrieving From Upstairs

If your dog will retrieve, place a favorite toy at the top of the stairs and send him after it. "Find your ball! Go stairs!"

You will need to help him with this combination at first, by running up or down with him. But soon he will come to trust that when you combine "Ball" and "Stairs," there really is a ball for him to find—and the STAIRS will take him to it.

Never lie to your dog—even accidentally. If you point him in the direction of the stairs and tell him his ball is that way, it had darned well better be there!

Because if he bounds up the stairs, trusting what you say and eagerly anticipating finding his ball…and it isn't there…he will begin to doubt your word.

So make sure you **know** that a particular toy is indeed where you tell him it is, before you send him for it.

Word #71: "Go Inside"

When you're outside in the yard with your dog, get his attention: "Jake!" With a dramatic wave of your arm, point toward the door of your house and hold your arm extended in that direction. "Go Inside. Inside."

Run toward the door yourself, encouraging your dog to accompany you. "Good boy! Go Inside." When you reach the door, open it and motion him through. "Inside. Good boy!"

It shouldn't be long before you can stand in the far corner of the yard, wave your arm toward the back door and call, "Go INside!" and your dog will make a beeline for the house.

"Inside" can also be used for any situation where you want your dog to go INTO some sort of enclosure.

"Go car. Inside. IN."

"Go crate. INside. IN."

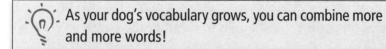

As your dog's vocabulary grows, you can combine more and more words!

Word #72: "Go Couch"
Word #73: "Go Chair"

Choose two pieces of furniture you don't mind your dog jumping on. Let's say a couch and an easy chair on opposite sides of the living room.

Get your dog's attention: "Jake!" With a dramatic wave of your arm, point toward the couch and hold your arm extended toward it. "Go couch. Couch!"

Run toward the couch, encouraging your dog to come with you. Motion for him to jump onto it. Hold a treat right over the couch if necessary, or take his collar and help him jump up. Give him the treat once he's up there.

Now it's only a matter of encouraging your dog to jump onto the couch without your needing to run all the way with him. Eventually you want to be able to stand across the room and send him onto the couch. Once he's up there, you can caution him to "Wait" while you go to him and give him his treat.

For variety, once he has jumped onto the couch and turned to face you, raise your arm in the Emergency Down signal and tell him, "Down!" When he lies down, count silently to five. Walk over and give him a treat. Make sure he holds his "Down." Caution him to "Stay," if necessary. Walk back to your original position. Count to five again. Then release him with "Okay!"

Go through the same routine when teaching, "Go chair!"

Then, just as you did when you sent your dog to fetch alternate toys (The Musical Toys Game), send him to the couch, then to the chair, then back to the couch. Sometimes give him a treat, sometimes just praise and petting. Sometimes ask him to "Down!" on the couch or chair. Sometimes send him directly from the couch or chair to his crate, or upstairs to fetch a toy.

Games! Variety! Dogs love 'em!

Heeling on your left side

Word #74: "Heel"

Let's talk now about a more formal type of walking, called **heeling**.

Heeling means your dog walks at your left side, with his head very close to your left leg. The leash hangs completely loose, forming a big U-shaped loop between your hand and his collar.

A heeling dog is very attentive to you. If you turn to the right or left, a heeling dog will turn with you, maintaining his position close beside your knee. If you slow down or speed up, a heeling dog will slow down or speed up, too. If you stop walking, a heeling dog will sit beside you and wait for your next move.

 A heeling dog is impressive to watch and very easy to walk!

Ah, but…is such a walk fun for him? For short periods, yes, it can be—especially when you make a game out of it, making quick turns, encouraging him to maintain his position, and praising him for his attentiveness.

 Heeling is a terrific exercise for teaching your dog to pay attention to you!

But as I mentioned in Chapter 13 (Walking and Exercise), on a normal walk you want your dog to have some freedom on the leash so he can sniff around a bit, and relieve himself if necessary. You don't want him to be so concerned about maintaining an exact position beside you that he can't even look around at the passing scenery.

For normal walks, I simply want my dog to walk without pulling on the leash. She can be in front of me, or behind me, or off to one side or the other. Just so long as she doesn't pull!

But there are times when you need more control, when you need your dog closer to you.

For example, if you have to walk through a crowd of people. Or if there is a dog or cat or squirrel nearby. Or if your arms are full of groceries and you can't be tripping over a dog walking in front of you or running back and forth from your left side to your right side. At these times, the word "Heel" comes in mighty handy.

Is your dog ready for heeling?

To **compete** with your dog in official obedience trials, the heeling exercise must be extremely precise—more so than what I'll be showing you here.

If you think you might have any interest in showing your dog in obedience competition, you need a book that teaches precision heeling. I recommend ***Beyond Basic Dog Training*** (by Diane Bauman).

But simple, non-competitive heeling is not difficult to teach—IF YOU CAN KEEP YOUR DOG'S ATTENTION.

If you've already taught your dog "Watch me!" (Word #30), if he looks at you when you say his name, if he maintains eye contact with you, you can move on to basic heeling.

Heeling "clues" you should give your dog

1. **Have your dog "Sit!" on your left side before you start to heel.** He should be facing the same direction you are, his head close to your left knee or ankle, depending on his size.

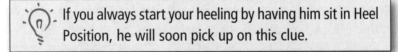

> If you always start your heeling by having him sit in Heel Position, he will soon pick up on this clue.

2. **Take your first heeling step with your LEFT foot.** Since he's sitting on your left, if you move your left foot he will immediately see it and can quickly rise from his sit and maintain his position walking beside you.
3. **Make your first step a small step.** This gives him more time to rise and keep up with you.

Starting to heel

1. With your dog sitting in the heeling position on your left side, call his name, "Jake!" When he looks up at you, say "Watch me!" and make sure he is focusing on you.

2. Say, "Jake, heel" and take your first step—a small step—with your left foot.

3. Walk only six or eight steps and keep his head from getting ahead of or behind your leg by using the technique you learned about in Chapter 13—the **Quick Tug and Relax**. (Go back and read about that technique if you need a quick refresher.)

Making an about turn

An about turn means turning and walking in the **opposite** direction.

Your about turn should be made to the RIGHT—away from your dog. As you turn, lower whichever hand is holding the leash to the level of your dog's head and use gentle tugs on the leash to guide your dog to make the turn with you. Keep walking as you turn—don't stand still and wait for your dog. Keep moving, and encourage him, "Keep up, Jake. Good boy!"

An alternative, if it works better for your particular dog, is to bend forward at the waist as you make the turn and pat your hands gently together, out in front of you and down low at your dog's eye level, to catch his eye. Encourage him, "Keep up, Jake! Good boy!"

After heeling a bit in the new direction, make another about turn and heel some more.

Stop heeling and have your dog sit

You're probably dizzy from all these about turns! Time to stop walking. But HOW you stop is very important:

1. Take a couple of short baby steps.
2. Plant your right foot in the ground and STOP moving it.
3. Bring your left foot slowly into position beside your planted right foot.

If you're consistent about it, the short baby steps, planting of your right foot, and slow movement of your left foot will all become clues to your dog that you're about to stop walking. This will help him stop with you.

AS you stop, say, "Sit." Pull up on the leash with your right hand and push down on your dog's hindquarters with your left hand so that he is sitting straight beside you, facing the same direction you are. Praise him!

If you're consistent about having him sit every time you stop walking, he will eventually start to sit as soon as you tug the leash upward, without your needing to say "Sit." Soon after that, he will start sitting before you have a chance to tug the leash OR say anything. This is called an **automatic sit** and it's a good thing.

> Heeling is mentally tiring for a dog. Practice for only two or three MINUTES at a time. You can always hold another two- or three-minute heeling session later in the day.

Fun heeling patterns

After awhile you'll get bored with walking in a straight line, making an about turn, and walking in another straight line. Try these different heeling patterns:

- Make a 90-degree turn to the left. Continue walking.
- Make a 90-degree turn to the right. Continue walking.
- Walk faster. Break into a trot, with short quick steps.
- Walk slower. Take l-o-n-g s-l-o-w steps, dragging out each step so your foot is in the air longer than usual. **Caution:** Don't take slow, short, baby steps or your dog will become confused. He'll anticipate that you're going to stop and he will keep trying to sit.
- Walk in circles. First large circles, fifteen feet across. Then smaller circles, five feet across. Circle to the right. Circle to the left.

- Combine two circles into a figure-8 pattern around two posts (or two chairs, two books, two rocks, two orange traffic cones) placed on the ground about eight feet apart.

Are we having fun yet?

Heeling on your right side

 "Why do dogs always heel on your LEFT side?"

A popular theory is that hunting dogs and guard dogs traditionally walked on the left side so the hunter or soldier could carry his weapon in his right hand.

In obedience competition, your dog always heels on your left side. But for practical purposes, your dog can learn to heel on both sides, as long as you use a different command for each side. If you use "Heel" for heeling on your left side, then for your right side try a command such as...

Word #75: "Right Side"

Start out with your dog heeling on your left side. As you're walking along, say cheerfully, "Jake, RIGHT side!"

Then do the following (read this carefully before you try it with your dog):

To switch your dog from one side to the other, make an about turn to your LEFT (the opposite direction from your usual about turn). As you turn, use the leash to guide your DOG into making an about turn to his RIGHT. Both of you continue heeling in the new direction, except that he's now on your right side.

Here's what it looks like:

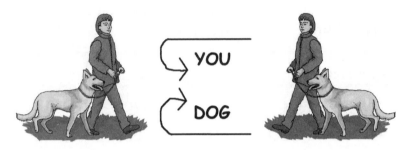

After you've made the switch, heel with your dog on your right side for a dozen steps, then say, "Jake, HEEL" and make another dual about turn, toward each other as before. This will put him back on your left side. Heel with him on your left side for a dozen steps, then switch again.

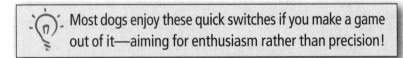

Most dogs enjoy these quick switches if you make a game out of it—aiming for enthusiasm rather than precision!

"Come Front" (come and sit in front of you)

Word #76: "Come Front"

When you call your dog and he comes to you, what happens when he **reaches** you?

Does he jump all over you? Frolic in circles around you? It's okay if he does! We've allowed him to do so. We just wanted him to COME.

But in obedience competition, when you call your dog, he must run to you and **sit directly in front of you**, facing you. This is a controlled position that can be very useful in everyday life, too. Sitting and facing you, your dog is focused on YOU rather than on whatever distraction you called him away from. Sometimes you need this kind of focus.

To tell your dog to come sit in front of you, facing you, we use the phrase "Come Front" instead of "Come."

You can use "Come Front":

- When you're calling your dog away from a distraction, so that once he gets to you, he has to concentrate on doing a proper sit and looking up at you, not at the distraction.
- When you need your dog close enough to put your hands on him—for example, to clip on his leash or pick him up.

Teaching "Come Front"

1. Stroll around the yard with your dog, on-leash. When his attention is elsewhere, call, "Jake, come FRONT." **Come** he already knows, so emphasize the new part of the phrase.
2. TROT backward. As he comes toward you, pat your hands together in encouragement and repeat, "Come FRONT. Come FRONT."
3. When he is at a good point just in front of you, STOP and use the leash to help hold him there in front of you. Have him sit in front of you, facing you.

   Once he is sitting, observe his position. Is he close enough to you that when you extend your arm straight out, your palm is directly over his head? If he's even closer than that, fine! You just don't want him further away than that.

   If he is sitting too far away or really crooked (you're facing north or south, while he's facing east or west), take a few more steps backward. Repeat, "Come FRONT" and try to get him sitting straighter, either using a treat to entice him into a better position, or the leash, or your hands.
4. Once he's sitting close enough and straight enough, praise him and release with "Okay!"

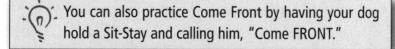 You can also practice Come Front by having your dog hold a Sit-Stay and calling him, "Come FRONT."

The Finish (return to heel position)

When your dog is sitting in front of you after "Come Front" and you want him to go to the heel position on your left side, this movement, in obedience competition, is called **The Finish**.

Let's say your dog is sitting in front of you, facing you. To go to heel position, there are two directions he can go.

1. He can move toward your left, which is a direct line to the heel position.
2. Or he can move toward your right, go around behind you, and come up into heel position.

We're going to teach your dog **both** of these directions and you'll be able to give him a command and hand signal telling him which way you want him to go. If you turn this exercise into a cheerful game, most dogs find it fun!

Word #77: "Swing"

This word will tell your dog to go to heel position by going directly to your left side.

1. With your dog sitting in front of you, facing you, reach out with your left hand and grasp the leash very close to his collar, as close to the snap as possible.
2. In a cheerful voice, tell your dog, "Swing!"
3. Take one large step backward with your left foot, sweeping your left hand and arm to the left and backward in a large arc, using the leash to guide your dog past your left leg so he is behind you, before turning him in a left about-turn so he is facing the same direction you are, with his head close beside your leg.
4. Use your hands to guide him into a sit in heel position.

Word #78: "Around"

This word will tell your dog to go to heel position by going to your right, behind you, and into heel position at your left.

1. With your dog sitting in front of you, facing you, reach out with your right hand and grasp the leash very close to his collar, as close to the snap as possible.
2. In a cheerful voice, tell your dog, "Around!"
3. Take one large step backward with your right foot, sweeping your right hand to the right and backward in an arc, using the leash to guide your dog past your right leg, and around behind you.
4. As he comes around behind you, switch the leash behind your back from your right hand to your left hand and step forward with your right foot so it's back where it started, as you smoothly continue to guide your dog up beside your left leg.
5. Use your hands to guide him into a sit in heel position.

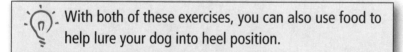 With both of these exercises, you can also use food to help lure your dog into heel position.

"But where are the hand signals?" you ask.

Ah, look closely! You're introducing them to your dog when you swing your left hand to the left, or your right hand to the right.

When you're first teaching these exercises, your hand is holding the leash, but eventually you'll be able to sweep your hand to the left or right—without holding or guiding the leash—and your dog will automatically move in the indicated direction!

Chapter 18

Fun Tricks

Most dogs love learning tricks. When they discover that certain behaviors make you laugh and applaud and reward them, they will even offer those behaviors on their own, hoping for a positive reaction from you. Dogs LIVE for this kind of attention!

Six Commandments For Teaching Tricks

- Offer treats.
- Practice for only two or three minutes at a time.
- Don't ask for the same trick more than three times.
- Praise and encourage the very beginnings of a trick.
- Guide your dog gently with your hands.
- No corrections when teaching tricks.

No corrections? Then why do we use corrections for other words such as "Come" and "Stay"? Because those words are essential, while tricks are optional bonus words.

> If you can guide and encourage your dog to do a particular trick and he enjoys doing it—great! If he doesn't seem to understand a trick, or can't do it, or doesn't like doing it—then simply don't ask him to do that trick.

So, without further ado, here are twelve popular tricks!

Shake hands

Word #79: "Shake Hands"

The classic dog trick. Even people who have never owned a dog will stretch their hand toward someone else's dog. "Hey, fella, wanna shake hands? Gimme a paw!"

Here's how to teach "Shake hands"

1. Have your dog sit in front of you, facing you. You may want to kneel down to be closer to his eye-level.
2. Extend your right hand, palm up, toward either of your dog's paws and in a cheerful voice, invite him to "Shake hands!" or "Give a paw!"
3. With the fingers of your right hand, tap (or tickle) the **back** of your dog's front leg, down near his ankle. When he lifts his paw, slide your right palm under his paw so his foot is resting on your palm. Don't grab or squeeze! Just let it rest on your hand. "Good boy!"
4. When he will lift his foot readily as you touch it, hold your hand NEAR his leg, but not touching it. Say, "Shake hands." If he lifts his paw without your needing to touch it, he has the idea.
5. With some dogs, you can progress to offering your hand higher and higher until finally you can stand in front of him and hold

out your palm and he'll lift his paw high to reach your hand. At this point, some owners switch to the phrase, "Gimme FIVE!"

An occasional dog is reluctant to shake. When you touch his paw, he'll pull it back. Or he'll raise it, but not want to rest it on your hand. He may be afraid that you're going to grab or squeeze. Be patient and gentle, but if he continues to resist this trick, don't push it on him.

Are you speaking to me?

Word #80: "Are You Speaking to Me?"

You've already taught your dog how to "Speak" (Word #41). It's a fine trick in and of itself, but here's a fun twist you can add.

When my dog Buffy woofs at me, politely, trying to tell me something or entice me to play, I ask, "Buffy, are you SPEAKing to me?"

She barks again, more enthusiastically.

"What are you SAYing?" I ask her, innocently. "What are you SAYing to me?"

"BARK, BARK!" she shouts happily.

Guests always get a kick out of this exchange!

At first you'll need to emphasize the key words: "Are you SPEAKing to me? What are you SAYing?" If your dog seems confused, you may need to prompt him with the simpler and more familiar "Speak. Speak." But soon he will learn the pattern of your phrases and won't need the prompting.

Dogs produce very different sounds in response to these phrases.

- Some dogs will offer a single sharp bark.
- Some dogs will unleash a series of barks.
- Hound dogs may produce a bay or howl.

Buffy makes a rolling, musical grumble (RR-rr, RR-rr, rr-rr-rr), like she's trying to converse with me. It's really cute!

If your dog offers an especially unusual sound, such as a howl or conversational grumble, you might try giving it a separate word, such as **SINGING**. Encourage your dog (with praise and treats) to reproduce it and attach "Sing" to it. Playing a musical instrument or certain recordings brings out the inner songster in some dogs!

> As with all tricks, there are some dogs who just won't do this one. They stand there mutely, staring at you as you cavort around and cajole them to "Speak! Speak!" until you feel like an idiot.

Crawl

Word #81: "Crawl"

If your dog can "Lie Down" and "Come," he may be able to "Crawl."

What is required for this trick is for your dog to lie down and creep forward, keeping his belly close to the ground while propelling himself toward you with his paws.

Many dogs will crawl. Police dogs crawl under fences. Search and rescue dogs crawl under obstacles. Terriers crawl through underground tunnels to reach their prey. Movie dogs, such as Lassie, are master crawlers, often whimpering pitifully as they creep toward the camera.

Here's how to teach "Crawl"

1. Have your dog lie down, either on your left side (in heel position), or in front of you (facing you). Experiment to find out which position works better with your dog.

2. Place your left hand on top of his shoulders. With your right hand, hold a treat just in front of your dog's nose and begin to draw it away from your dog, wiggling it in an enticing manner—but keep it close to the ground so he will keep his head close to the ground, too. Hold his shoulders down gently so he can't stand up. Draw out the word, "Cra-a-a-w-l?" in a long, slow, coaxing tone.

   If he manages to push past your restraining hand and stands up, just replace him in the down position. No corrections. "Down...good boy. Cra-a-a-w-l?"

3. If he wriggles forward, even just an inch or two, praise him enthusiastically and give him the treat. In the beginning, you want to reward even the slightest glimmer of understanding and effort. Eventually extend the distance he needs to crawl before you give him the treat.

 You can teach some dogs to crawl under a chair or low table, or even under someone's legs!

A potential problem with this trick is that some dogs become less reliable doing a Down-Stay. Once they learn to crawl, you see, they're tempted to try it when they're supposed to be lying down and staying. If this happens with your dog, I would drop this trick from his repertoire. A reliable Down-Stay is more valuable than being able to crawl.

Play dead

Word #82: "Play Dead" (or "Go To Sleep" or "Naptime")

1. Have your dog "Sit" and "Stay" while you face him from a foot or two away.
2. Form a "gun" with your right hand by pointing your right index finger at your dog, your other three fingers curled into your palm, your thumb sticking straight up. Say, "Bang!" or "Play dead!" as you jerk your hand up like you've just shot him.
3. Step forward quickly—but not threateningly as if you're going to correct him! Gently guide your dog into a down position and then roll him flat onto his side, repeating "Bang" or "Play dead" as you do so. Hold his head gently on the floor for just a second of two, repeating, "Play dead! Good boy."
4. Then say happily, "You're ALIVE!" and encourage him to jump up and get his treat.

If you don't like the idea of "shooting" your dog, just substitute the more peaceful "NAP time" or "Take a NAP" or "Go to SLEEP" combined with "Wake up!" as the release word. As a hand signal for this version, place your palms together as though in prayer and rest them against the side of your face like a child going nighty-night.

> This trick has practical uses. If your dog will lie flat on his side, it's easier to examine his stomach for fleas or burrs or groom tangled hair.

Roll over

Word #83: "Roll Over"

"Roll over" seems like a simple extension of playing dead...

But many dogs can't do it. Giving that extra little push to roll themselves completely over is difficult for many dogs and impossible for some.

Body tension is the most common obstacle. A rolling dog needs to be **relaxed** so his spine is supple and flexible enough to roll. If your dog feels stressed or nervous, he will tighten up and then this trick will become impossible.

Here's how to teach "Roll over"

1. Have your dog lie down, either on your left side (in heel position), or in front of you (facing you). Experiment to find out which position works better with your dog.

   Now, there's something you need to observe here. When a dog is lying down, his front legs are stretched in front of him, while his hind legs stick out to one side or the other.

   Notice whether your dog's hind legs are sticking out on his **left** side or on his **right** side.

2. Kneel beside him. Hold a treat an inch in front of his nose. Say, "Roll over!" and start moving the treat slowly on a straight line from his nose toward his elbow so that he must turn his head to follow it. (This must be the elbow on the same side of his body as his hind legs are sticking out.) As he follows the treat, his nose will move toward his outstretched back feet. Then lift your hand up so it crosses over his head—toward the opposite side from his back legs.

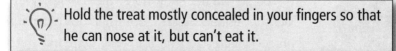

Hold the treat mostly concealed in your fingers so that he can nose at it, but can't eat it.

3. As his head turns to follow the treat, his body will tilt **away** from the treat and partway into a roll. Place your other hand (the hand without the treat) on his shoulder to push him further over onto his back and hip—and at the same time maneuver your treat hand in such a way as to LURE him into rolling over the rest of the way.

    It's very hard to describe the correct motion—you have to try it yourself to get the knack of it!

4. As soon as your dog makes it over, even if you have to roll him yourself, give him the treat and lots of praise.

Only ask your dog to roll over on soft surfaces like carpet or grass, or on your bed if he's small. NEVER ask him to roll over on concrete or on a wooden or vinyl floor—these are too hard on his back and spine.

> Remember, this is a difficult trick for many dogs, and an impossible trick for some. If your dog can't do it, or doesn't like it, skip it and move on to something else.

Beg

Word #84: "Beg"

This is an old-fashioned trick that some dogs do easily. Other dogs can't do it at all, because sitting upright on their hindquarters requires them to hold their backbone firmly erect, plus maintain a good sense of balance.

You should not allow dogs with a long back (like Dachshunds and Basset Hounds) to do this trick—it puts too much stress on the weak vertebrae in their long spine.

Here's how to teach "Beg"

1. Have your dog sit, facing you. Some owners find it helpful to put large dogs in a corner—facing OUT, of course, duh! The walls help provide support for balancing.

2. Hold a treat just above your dog's head and say, "Beg" in a cheerful voice. If your dog tries to get the treat by rocking back on his hindquarters and lifting his front paws off the ground, even just a little bit, give him the treat and praise him.

   You need to hold the treat at just the right spot over his nose for him to sit firmly on his haunches and balance properly. You'll have to experiment to find the right spot for your dog. If you hold the treat too high, he'll stand up on his hind legs rather than rocking back onto his haunches.

3. If you can't seem to lure your dog into lifting his front feet, you may need to lift his front legs yourself, rocking him slightly backward so that he settles onto his hindquarters. You can drape his feet lightly over your wrist or forearm to help him balance. Or try putting your hand under his chin to help him balance.

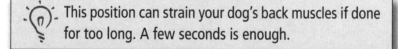 This position can strain your dog's back muscles if done for too long. A few seconds is enough.

Dance

Word #85: "Dance"

Dancing is different from begging. Begging asks your dog to sit up on his hindquarters and wait for you to give him the treat, while dancing asks your dog to stand up on his toes and waltz around, actively trying to solicit the treat.

Here's how to teach "Dance"

1. Hold a treat just above your dog's head and say, "Dance! Dance!" When he reaches for it, raise it higher and wiggle it around to entice him to rise up on his toes and stretch for it.

   You'll need to hold the treat higher than you do for "Beg," because you want him to stand up on his toes. But not TOO high, or he'll get frustrated and will simply bark at you or give up.

2. At first, as soon as he extends himself even a little bit, give him the treat and praise him. Gradually coax him to stay up longer and dance around more. Repeat, "Dance! Good boy! Dance!" as he's sashaying around.

3. As with begging, if the treat isn't enough to lure your dog into standing up on his toes, lift him up yourself. Once he's up on his toes, hold his paws very gently (don't squeeze!) or drape his front feet over your wrist and waltz around with him.

> I sing the old Australian folk song "Waltzing Matilda" when I dance with my dog. No, I don't feel silly at all. Well, okay, maybe a little silly.

Circle (Spin)

Word #86: "Circle" (or "Spin")

All your dog has to do for this trick is to turn around in a tight little circle. Many dogs get so excited doing this trick that they chase their tail!

Here's how to teach "Circle"

With your dog standing in front of you, show him a treat. Say, "Circle!" and lead his nose with the treat so that he turns in a tight circle. When he has made one full revolution (so that he's facing you again), praise him and give him the treat.

When he will turn readily around being led by the treat, try motioning him in a circle with your treat hand, without actually putting it in front of his nose. "Circle!"

 HINT: Always turn your dog in the same direction, and make sure your hand motion is in that SAME direction.

Kiss

Word #87: "Give A Kiss"

Some dogs love this trick, while others refuse to do it. Many dogs will kiss their family, but not a stranger.

For those who like it, it's easy to teach. Whenever your dog licks your face on his own, say, "Give me a kiss!" You can encourage him by dabbing a little peanut butter on your cheek!

> **Caution:** YOU might think that being licked by a dog is wonderful, but many other people do not like to be licked. If you share your home with such people, I recommend that you don't teach this trick, because it's hard for a dog to remember who he can kiss, and who he can't. Remember the value of consistent rules!

> -ʘ- Also keep in mind that some people are allergic to canine
> saliva and can end up with a runny nose, runny eyes,
> or stuffed head from a simple kiss.

Catch

Word #88: "Catch"

When giving a treat to your dog, you don't always have to hand it to him. You can toss it to him and he can catch it in mid-air, like this.

Well, okay, maybe not exactly like this!

To teach your dog to catch a treat (or a toy)

1. Position yourself so you're about a foot away from your dog. Once he notices that you have a treat, he will naturally try to get closer to you, so you may have to dance around a bit to create some space between the two of you.
2. Hold up the treat so he sees it. Say, "Catch!" and toss the treat gently toward his mouth.
3. Be ready to move! Because if it bonks him on the head or falls to the ground, you need to grab it with your hand or cover it with your foot before he can snatch it up. He should only get the treat if he catches it. I know, I know...this is easier said than done!

   Some dogs have excellent eye-mouth coordination and learn this trick quickly. Other dogs take much longer. With a reluctant dog, try kneeling right in front of him, holding your hand only a few inches from his mouth and tossing it from there. Aim right for his mouth, which may encourage him to make a token grab for the oh-so-close treat.

> Some dogs are really uncomfortable when you toss anything toward them. If your dog is intimidated by a tossed treat, this is not the trick for him. Don't frighten him.

Back up

Word #89: "Back Up"

"Back up" is one of the most practical tricks because there are many times when you want your dog to move backward a few steps.

- He may have followed you across your property line or through a gate.
- He may be too close to a delicate project you're working on, or to a potentially dangerous object.
- He may be too close to something he might frighten, such as your parakeet.

In all of these cases, moving backward a bit would put him in a better or safer position.

Here's how to teach "Back up"

With your dog standing in front of you, show him this new hand signal: Hold your hand about a foot in front of your waist, palm facing you and fingers pointing toward the floor. Now, keeping your wrist still, bend your hand and fingers away from you and then back toward you in a SLOWLY repeated flicking motion, as though shooing away a pesky critter.

> Be sure to make this motion slowly. A more vigorous flicking motion belongs to the "Shoo!" command (Word #36).

As you motion him backward with your hand signal, say, "Back up. Back. Back." Take a few small steps toward him and repeat, "Back up. Back. Back." You're trying to crowd him so he'll step back.

If he takes even one step backward, praise him and give him a treat.

If he knows how to "Catch" (Word #88), you can toss him the treat instead of handing it to him. Then you don't have to walk toward him, and he won't be tempted to run toward you. He can stay wherever he backed up to, and still receive his treat.

If instead of backing up in a fairly straight line, he repeatedly tries to sidestep you when you move toward him, practice in a hallway or other narrow passageway where he doesn't have much room to maneuver. If the only direction he can go is back, he'll learn it more quickly.

Over time, you'll want him to keep backing up as long as you keep flicking your wrist. And you'll want to cut down on stepping toward him and rely more on your hand motion and your voice to "back him up."

If time goes by, and he still won't respond without your stepping toward him, hold a lightweight stick or fly swatter vertically beside your leg. As you give him your hand signal and tell him to "Back up," raise the lower tip of the stick and poke or tap him lightly on his foot or leg. That may do the trick!

Say Yes

Word #90: "Say Yes"

What seems like a simple trick of your dog nodding his head up and down can be made into a real performance if you're willing to play it up.

"Buffy, I think the Bruins will win the Stanley Cup this year, don't you? Say YES!"

And of course your dog nods her head in agreement!

This is an easy trick to teach—but not necessarily an easy one to learn. That sounds cryptic, I know, but it just means that the teaching technique is obvious—you move a treat up and down so that your dog's head does the same thing—and yet many dogs won't progress to doing it without the treat. Perhaps the nodding motion is not natural enough to them. But it's such a great parlor trick that it's worth a try.

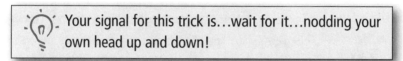 Your signal for this trick is...wait for it...nodding your own head up and down!

Wave

Word #91: "Wave"

This is an extension of Shake Hands (Word #79). Once your dog will place his paw in your palm, you can progress to holding your palm outstretched and changing the command to "Wave." The familiar signal of your outstretched palm will probably be enough for him to lift his paw, and as soon as he does, praise him and give a treat.

Once he is reliably sitting still and lifting his paw, change your hand signal from an outstretched palm (which belongs to Shake Hands) to a more wiggly motion like an actual wave.

He will understand this transition more quickly if you offer the new hand signal (the waving hand) right before the old hand signal (the outstretched hand). In other words, you "morph" the new signal into the old to give him confidence that he is doing the right thing and eventually you fade out the old signal entirely.

Weave

Word #92: "Weave"

Wait, didn't we just do this one? Not exactly. Word #91 was **WAVE**. Word #92 is **WEAVE**.

In this trick, your dog does a figure-8 pattern through and around your legs, like so...

From a starting position in front of you, he walks between your legs, veers to his left and comes around your right leg, then walks between your legs again and veers to his right to come around your left leg, ending up in front of you again.

A figure-8 pattern.

How do you get him to do this? With treats! You're going to lure him through the pattern with a treat held in front of his nose. "Weave. Good boy. Weave."

You'll actually want two treats, one in each hand.

1. With the treat in your right hand, put that hand **behind** your right thigh and then move your arm over to your buttocks so the treat is visible to your dog between your legs. Use it to entice your dog through your legs and around your right leg. When he reaches his original position in front of you, give him the treat.
2. Now use the treat in your left hand to do the same thing on the other side.
3. Keep encouraging him to "Weave" as you coax him through the entire figure-8 pattern.

> It's possible to do this trick as part of the "Heel" exercise (Word #74). However, your dog must be able to heel off-leash because he needs to weave through your legs as you both walk. Very impressive!

Chapter 19

Doggy Obstacle Course

The sport of Dog Agility

Over the hurdles! Up the ramp! Across the plank! Down the ramp! Through the tunnel! Up the climbing wall! Down the climbing wall! Across the teeter-totter!

Is this a playground? Yes, a playground for dogs. **Dog Agility** is an obstacle course for dogs—and dogs love it!

The next time you sign onto the Internet, check out this terrific animation of Dog Agility:

www.yourpurebredpuppy.com/ebooks/agilityanimation.html

In Dog Agility, your dog runs around the obstacle course, off-leash. He climbs on, over, and under the obstacles. You run beside him, directing him toward the next obstacle. He must follow your directions at all times.

The obstacles are arranged in different patterns. Beginning dogs run on simple courses, while advanced dogs run on more challenging courses.

As you might expect, the best dogs for Agility are those who are lively and athletic. However, Agility can be enjoyed even by overweight dogs, and by deformed dogs like Dachshunds, Bassets, Great Danes, and

Pugs—IF you set the obstacles at a very low height and simply WALK your dog through the course, perhaps even on-leash.

Cautions!

- Be especially considerate of elderly dogs. Their eyesight and balance may be failing and though they may be enthusiastic about trying the course, you must constantly monitor them for safety and be prepared to physically assist them.
- Dogs with health problems, such as heart disease or arthritis or hip dysplasia, should be cleared by your vet. Some of these dogs will be okay as long as you pick out a few simple obstacles, set them at the lowest possible height, and walk your dog over them on-leash.
- Puppies and adolescent dogs should NEVER be allowed to run through an obstacle course full-speed or jump over anything higher than six inches. Their bones and joints are still growing and can be seriously, perhaps irreparably, damaged by too much running or jumping.

What's so great about Dog Agility?

Agility provides a constructive physical outlet for your dog's energy and enthusiasm.

Agility requires your dog to think and pay attention. He must follow your directions, remember the names of the different obstacles, and remember how to negotiate each obstacle.

Agility builds self-confidence. Learning to conquer challenging obstacles and (if you go to a public agility class) performing in a new environment in front of strangers are valuable skills that will carry over to other areas of your dog's life.

If you own a timid or nervous dog, definitely try Agility to boost his confidence and bring him out of his shell.

Agility makes you and your dog true partners. You have to work closely with your dog, which creates a healthy bond between the two of you.

You can compete in agility

Agility is the fastest-growing dog sport in the United States. You'll often see it on TV on *Animal Planet*. Spectators love watching the enthusiasm of the dogs as they race against the clock.

In an Agility trial, each Owner-Dog pairing runs through the course individually. In each size division, the winner is the pairing with the fastest time and the fewest faults (penalties for knocking over a jump, refusing an obstacle, taking an obstacle out of turn, etc.).

To find agility clubs in your area, search Google™ online for "agility clubs."

What happens in an Agility class?

Your dog will be introduced to the obstacles, which will be set very low. The goal is to build his confidence by showing him that the obstacles are really a piece of cake!

Agility class resembles a gymnastics class. You walk or trot your dog over an obstacle and the instructor and his assistants stand alongside as "spotters" to make sure your dog doesn't fall.

Since a leash throws off his balance, it needs to come off very soon so your dog can progress from walking and trotting to all-out running.

Therefore, to take part in an Agility class, your dog must be reliable off-leash. He must come back to you when you call him, and he must not be aggressive toward people or other dogs.

Very few corrections are used in an Agility class. Instead, you entice your dog with treats and praise, guide him with your hands, and make the whole experience light-hearted and fun.

Once your dog learns the basic obstacles

- The height, length, or steepness of each obstacle will be slowly increased.
- Obstacles will be set up in sequence so your dog must do several in a row instead of just one. In competition, a course includes over a dozen obstacles.
- You'll learn the voice commands and hand signals to direct your dog around the course.

An Introductory or Beginner's Class usually runs eight to twelve weeks. Then you move on to Intermediate and Advanced classes—and perhaps on to competition.

If I join an Agility class, do I have to compete in a trial?

No, absolutely not! You and your dog can simply take the classes and have fun with the training.

You can even skip the classes entirely and buy or build your own obstacles at home.

However, obstacles can be dangerous if you don't build them solidly enough, or if you allow your dog to perform an obstacle incorrectly. Obstacles can collapse. Dogs can fall or pull muscles. Dogs can be injured doing Agility.

If you're going to build your own obstacles, I strongly recommend that you buy step-by-step plans that include exact measurements. Or buy ready-made obstacles. Visit *www.affordableagility.com* and *www.agilitykits.com*.

Now let's look at eight basic obstacles.

Jumps and hurdles

Word #93: "Jump" (or "Over")

Jumps can be solid hurdles, or they can be bar jumps—two vertical posts holding one or more horizontal bars.

You can build bar jumps out of plastic PVC pipe, which is lightweight and inexpensive. However, white PVC is hard for your dog to see, so buy some brightly colored contact paper, cut it into strips, and wrap the colored strips around the white pipe at spaced intervals.

Jumps are usually arranged in sequence—your dog jumps several in succession. So build or buy at least three jumps.

How high to set jumps

You never set the height of a jump based on how high your dog CAN jump—but on how high he SHOULD jump.

- Your dog needs to develop his muscles for jumping.
- He must learn when to take off and how to land safely.
- He must learn a comfortable rhythmic stride between jumps.

When you're teaching your dog to jump properly, jump heights should be set very low so he can concentrate on these critical skills.

How low? One formula says to keep jumps set at the height of your dog's elbow—or 12 inches—**whichever number is LESS.**

Another formula says to keep jumps set at HALF the height your dog would need to jump in competition. Depending on which organization is running the trial, your adult dog would need to jump, roughly:

Height of dog at shoulder	Height of jump
Dog up to 10"	Jump 8"
Dog 10" to 14"	Jump 8" to 12"
Dog 14" to 18"	Jump 16" to 22"
Dog 18" to 22"	Jump 20" to 24"
Dog over 22"	Jump 24" to 26"

Even after he is a skilled and experienced jumper, your dog should not practice at these competition heights or he'll wear out his joints. HALF his competition height is plenty enough for regular practice.

Keep those jumps low!

Extreme caution: puppies and adolescent dogs

Most owners are not aware of how fragile the bones and joints are in growing puppies and adolescent dogs. Until their expanding growth plates have stopped growing and are fully closed, jumping too high can severely damage them, sometimes irreparably.

Ironically, it is the impact of LANDING after the jump that causes the most stress on the bones and joints.

When do the growth plates close? It varies by breed. For most breeds under 50 pounds, growth plates close around 9–12 months. For most breeds over 50 pounds, growth plates close around 10–14 months.

Until their growth plates have closed,
a puppy should only jump
his height at the elbow, or 12 inches—
whichever number is LESS.

Secure footing is essential

More dogs are injured during their take-offs and landings than during the actual jump. They either slip on a surface that's too slick or they come down hard on a surface that's too rigid and unforgiving.

1. Make sure the area in front of the jump, where your dog will be pushing off the ground, has secure footing.

2. Make sure the area behind the jump, where your dog will be landing, has secure footing AND is soft and cushioned.

That means

- soft grass
- cushioned rubber matting
- cushioned carpeting securely fastened to the floor

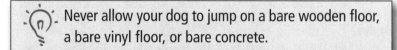 Never allow your dog to jump on a bare wooden floor, a bare vinyl floor, or bare concrete.

Teaching jumping

1. Place two or three jumps about ten feet apart. Set each jump only a few inches high.
2. With your dog on leash, WALK over the series of jumps with him. Reward with a treat when you've cleared the last jump. Repeat your walk several times—and that's enough for the day.
3. Eventually you will TROT over the jumps with him. Then you'll run.
4. Finally, run toward the jump with him, but at the last second you veer **around** the side of the jump while he goes over himself.

The major mistake made by impatient owners is to take their dog off-leash too soon. An off-leash dog can easily veer around the jump—and once this bad habit has been introduced to his brain, it can be very difficult to cure. Be patient! Keep your dog on-leash until his brain has formed the rock-solid pattern that "Jump" always means OVER—and never around.

Pause Table

Word #94: "Go Table"

The Pause Table is a small platform, three feet square, set on four sturdy legs 8 to 24 inches high, depending on your dog's size. You tell your dog "Go table!" and he jumps onto it, whereupon you tell him to "Sit" or "Down." He holds that position for five seconds, then you send him on to the next obstacle.

The Pause Table is a control exercise, so I don't recommend teaching it to puppies. Puppies should be encouraged to move and play in agility. Too much control too early will diminish their enthusiasm.

Teaching your dog to jump on the table

Make absolutely sure the table is covered with securely-fastened, non-slip carpeting or rubber matting.

1. Pat the table with your hand, tell your dog in a cheerful voice, "Go TABLE!" and hold a treat above it. When your dog jumps onto the table, place the treat ON the table so he can eat it.
2. Caution him, "Wait…wait…" (Word #32) while you count silently to five. Then release him with "Okay!" (Word #12) and encourage him to jump off the table.
3. After he has had some practice with this, place a treat ON the table so he can see it. Take him by the collar and lead him about six feet away. Turn him toward the table and encourage him, "Go table!" Release his collar and run to the table with him. He will probably beat you there and jump up to eat the treat, but if he doesn't, pat the table to encourage him to jump up. "Go table!"

    Each time you practice this, hang further back so he is running to the table without you needing to run beside him. Gradually extend your distance until you can send him to the table from a good twenty feet away!

Remember to have him "Wait" for five seconds before saying "Okay" and letting him jump off. At this point, he doesn't need to sit or lie down—he just needs to stay up there without jumping off.

4. Place a low hurdle in his path. Tell him, "Go table!" and make sure he jumps the hurdle on his way to the table. You may need to put him on-leash at first.

5. Finally, instead of placing a treat on the table beforehand, keep it in your pocket and simply send your dog to the table. When he jumps up, looking for the treat, do the Emergency Down. Raise your right arm high in the air and say, "Down!" When your dog hits the deck, caution him to "Stay" and then trot over and give him his treat.

> Never reward your dog for jumping OFF the table. If he jumps off before you reach him, say "Ah-Ah! Go table!" Only give him his treat ON the table so he learns to get up there and stay put.

Dogwalk

Word #95: "Walk It"

The dogwalk is really a catwalk—but of course, as a matter of pride, we can't call it that!

It's a wide balance beam (ten inches wide) with a ramp at each end. The beam is three or four feet off the ground. The two ramps and the central plank are each twelve feet long, so the whole obstacle is 36 feet in total length. Your dog walks up one ramp, walks along the central plank, and walks down the far ramp.

> Stepping on and off the ramps at the very bottom is mandatory. Your dog may not leap onto the Up ramp so that he starts halfway up it, and he may not come halfway down the Down ramp, then leap to the ground. This is unsafe!

In fact, it is so important that your dog step on and off each ramp properly, that the first three feet of the Up ramp, and the last three feet of the Down ramp are painted a bright color (usually yellow). This area is called a **contact zone.** Your dog must step on the contact zone on the way UP and on the way DOWN.

Teaching the dogwalk

1. Ignore the ramps at first. Simply lay the central plank flat on the ground and encourage your dog to walk its length. Keep his leash on to guide him.

2. Next, rest the plank on supports a few inches high. Keep the leash nice and loose so he can balance himself as he crosses the plank.

    When you're first teaching the dogwalk, don't use any commands. That sounds odd, but this is a new exercise and if your dog is at all nervous, he may connect whatever word you say with his fearful feelings. Then whenever you say the word, his automatic response may be to become nervous.

    So just walk your dog over the plank again and again, with only praise and encouragement. Once he shows understanding and confidence, begin adding the phrase "Walk it."

3. Next, your dog will learn the Down ramp. Prop one end of the ramp on your Pause Table. Set the other end of the ramp on the floor.

Since the ramp is not affixed to anything, you'll need a helper to hold it securely in place. If it suddenly plunked to the ground while your dog was walking on it, it would be too low to hurt him physically, but psychologically, it would be very bad and he might never want to walk on it again.

4. Place a **target** (for example, a paper plate or plastic lid) at the bottom of the ramp, on the floor. Place a treat on the target and position the target so that, when your dog stops to eat the treat, his front feet will be on the floor while his back feet are still on the ramp. This helps teach him to stay on the ramp all the way to the bottom.

5. Once your dog has mastered going down to eat his treat, have him go UP the ramp to a target ON the table. Then put a ramp on each side of the table and have him go up one ramp and down the other.

6. Now you're ready to graduate to the real dogwalk.

    If your dog is small, pick him up and place him halfway down the Down ramp. Have him simply walk down to the target (and treat!) at the bottom.

    With larger dogs, place the pause table beside the Down ramp at the point where the table is about level with the ramp. Have your dog jump onto the table, then encourage him to step onto the Down ramp and proceed down the ramp to the target at the bottom.

> Once your dog sees that he can walk DOWN this "Great Big" dogwalk, he will be more confident about going UP the ramp, across the central plank, and down the other side.

Doing the dogwalk with puppies

Puppies can do the dogwalk IF they have enough physical coordination to balance on the plank.

But I recommend focusing your puppy on the **CONTACT ZONES**. Use a puppy-sized plank—a generous 24 inches wide and only six feet long. Paint the contact zones (the first two feet and the last two feet) bright yellow. Leave the center of the plank unpainted.

1. Prop some bricks or a cement block under each end of the plank so it's raised up a few inches off the ground.
2. Now teach your puppy that the contact zones are where the treats are! Lure him onto one contact and have him sit there while he eats a treat.
3. Have someone else show him a treat at the other end of the plank. When he walks across, have him sit there and eat the treat.

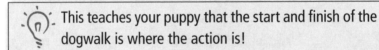

This teaches your puppy that the start and finish of the dogwalk is where the action is!

A-frame

Word #96: "Climb It"

The A-frame is a sloped climbing wall shaped like the letter A, with a peak about 5 or 5½ feet high. Your dog goes up one side of the A and down the other side.

Each incline is three feet wide, and eight or nine feet long. The inclines are hinged together with chain to form the A shape. Narrow wooden slats nailed horizontally onto each incline provide secure footing as your dog scrambles up one side, over the peak, and down the other side.

As with the dogwalk, the objective of the A-frame is not just to scale it—but to touch those contact zones at the bottom of each incline. Your dog is not allowed to leap onto the UP incline above the yellow contact zone—nor can he jump off the DOWN incline after coming only partway down.

Teaching the A-frame

1. Lower the A-frame until it is nearly flat, with only a very slight incline that your dog can literally walk over. Use the new command "Climb it."
2. After several such walk-overs, adjust the chains to make the angle steeper, which boosts the peak to two or three feet high.
3. Now teach the contact zones, just as you did with the dogwalk. This means using a target and treat to encourage your dog to walk all the way to the bottom of the incline, rather than jumping off halfway down.

To teach contact zones, place your small- or medium-sized dog halfway down the Down incline and have him walk down to a target at the bottom.

With larger dogs, place the pause table beside the Down incline and have your dog jump onto the table, step onto the incline, and proceed down the ramp to the target at the bottom.

> Remember to position the target so when your dog eats the treat, his front feet are on the ground while his rear feet are still on the incline.

4. Gradually place your dog higher and higher on the Down incline so that he is coming down further each time. Soon he will be

near the top, coming all the way down. Then place him on the peak itself. Then on the Up incline just beyond the peak, so he has to clamber over the peak and then down.

5. Finally, he will be ready for a **run by**. Put his leash on and lead him about ten feet from the A-frame. Focus his attention on the obstacle—make sure he is looking right at it. Encourage him to "Climb it!" and run with him toward the A-frame. Make sure he commits to it (is clearly focused on the incline and heading up it) before you run around the side to meet him on his way down. Keep that leash nice and loose so you don't throw him off-balance.

> The major problem with the A-frame is impatient owners making the peak too high. For virtually all practice sessions, the peak should stay at four feet high. On a steeper slope, your dog has to fight gravity coming down, which makes him more likely to start jumping off. Bad!

Puppies should only do the A-frame set at TWO feet high. In other words, they should be able to run over it without needing to "climb" at all. As with the dogwalk, focus on contacts—your puppy gets treats on the contact zones.

Tunnel

Word #97: "Go Tunnel"

You've seen children's play tunnels. Most of them are made of very cheap and flimsy vinyl, but Toys R Us® sells (or used to sell) a nice nylon tunnel that's higher quality yet still inexpensive. It's only six feet long, but if you buy two of them and hook them together, it makes a pretty good dog agility tunnel for smallish and midsized dogs. It even folds up into a compact hoop for easy storage.

You can also buy a regulation tunnel from an agility equipment manufacturer. I recommend a 15-foot tunnel. Much shorter, and you'll find it difficult to bend the tunnel into the traditional "U" or "S" shape.

For variety, you can make short homemade tunnels out of trash cans with the bottom cut out, or out of open-ended refrigerator cartons.

Teaching the tunnel

1. Compress the tunnel until it's only three feet long. Have a helper hold your dog by the collar at one end of the tunnel while you crouch at the opposite end. Stick your head inside and call, "Jake, here I am, Jake!" Wave a treat inside the tunnel to get his attention. You want him to peer in and make eye contact with you. When he does, call him, "Jake, come!" If he even sticks his head in, encourage him, "Yay! Good boy!"

2. Once he's all the way in, your helper should block the entrance so your dog can't suddenly change his mind and try to back out. Once he's in, whatever you have to do, he MUST come out the other side. When he reaches you, he gets praise and a treat.

3. Once your dog is going through without hesitation, gradually extend the length of the tunnel. Be sure to brace it securely along both sides so it can't roll while your dog is inside, which could really spook him.

4. Finally, he will be ready for a **run by**. Put his leash on and lead him about ten feet from the tunnel. Focus his attention on the obstacle. "See the tunnel? Go tunnel!" and RUN with

him toward the tunnel. Make sure he commits to it (has fully entered it at a good pace) before you run around the side to meet him on his way out.

> The most common problem with the tunnel is when your dog changes his mind and comes out the way he went in. Once established, this bad habit is difficult to break. The moral is: When teaching the tunnel, always use a helper who can block the entrance!

5. When your dog is completely confident about negotiating a straight tunnel, curve it into a "U" shape. This is psychologically difficult for many dogs because they can't see any light at the other end. They have to enter the dark end and trust that there will be an exit.

6. Finally, curve the tunnel into an "S" shape.

> Tunnels are perfect obstacles for puppies, and also for adult dogs with physical limitations who can't jump or climb well.

Chute

Word #98: "Go Chute"

The chute is simply a collapsed tunnel. One end is an open barrel, two feet long, which turns into a twelve-foot length of lightweight fabric material spread out on the ground. Your dog enters the open barrel and dashes under the fabric, lifting it up and making it ripple as he runs under it and out the far end.

For some dogs, the chute can be intimidating, because when they peer into the open barrel, the "tunnel" peters out into the ground. Your dog must learn through experience that he really can push his way under the fabric and emerge at the other end.

Other dogs, like my dog Buffy, love the sensation of running under the fabric. In fact, the chute is her all-time favorite obstacle. (These are often the same dogs who love burrowing under the bedcovers!)

Making a chute

Like other obstacles, chutes can be bought, or made at home. For the barrel part, you could use a heavy-duty plastic or rubber trash can with the solid end sawed off. Sand or tape any jagged edges, or attach foam padding all around the entrance. Attach non-skid rubber strips or matting inside the bottom of the barrel for secure footing. Finally, make sure the barrel rests in a sturdy cradle for stability.

For the chute fabric, you might sew plain bed sheets together, but the best material, by far, is midweight nylon. It's durable, water-resistant, and doesn't stretch or twist when dogs run through it. Don't use stretchy fabrics such as knit, or super-lightweight fabrics such as ripstop nylon. Where it attaches to the barrel, the fabric should be six feet wide, while the free end flares out to eight feet wide. You can secure the fabric to the barrel with wrap-around bungee cords.

Teaching the chute

1. First your dog should simply run through the barrel, so fold up the fabric around the barrel so it doesn't block your dog in any way. As you did when teaching the tunnel, have a helper hold your dog by the collar at one end of the barrel, while you call him through the other end.

2. When you begin extending the fabric, hold it up in the air and wide open with your hands at first, so your dog can still see you at the other end. He simply has to run through the open fabric to reach you.

3. Continue to extend the chute until your dog is running through the full twelve feet when it's wide open and held up off the ground. Then begin lowering your end of the chute when your dog is about three-quarters of the way through. He will feel it touch his shoulders and back as he runs through the last quarter. As he gains confidence that this "thing" is not going to smother him, lower the chute when he is halfway through, then one-quarter of the way through, and so on.

4. Finally he will be ready for a **run by** from about ten feet away. Focus your dog on the chute. "See chute? Go chute!" Make sure he commits to the chute before you release his collar. As always, have a helper standing by to block the entrance to the barrel so your dog can't change his mind.

Tire jump

Word #99: "Go Tire"

The tire jump, which is a tire suspended off the ground between supports, is a combination of a jump and a tunnel. The opening of the tire is 20–24 inches wide, and its height off the ground is whatever height your dog has to jump for other jumps.

Any hoop can form the tire. If you use a real car tire, tape it closed all around so your dog can't catch his foot in the slit when he jumps through.

The trickiest part of homemade tire construction is making it adjustable. You need to set the tire low for teaching purposes, and raise it only an inch or two at a time until you reach full height.

To make the tire adjustable, handy people have used chains, airline cable, hooks, eyelets, and cleats.

Or you can just buy one from an agility equipment manufacturer such as *www.affordableagility.com* or *www.agilitykits.com*.

Teaching the tire jump

First you need to convince your dog that he can indeed fit through this strange circle!

1. Hang the tire only a couple of inches off the ground.
2. Have a helper hold your dog by the collar on one side of the tire while you go to the other side. Establish eye contact with your dog through the opening of the tire, pat the bottom of the tire, and encourage your dog to hop through.
3. Once he is coming through without hesitation with you on the opposite side of the tire, progress to **run bys** from about ten feet away, where you run with your dog to the tire and send him through while you go around it. Focus your dog on the tire first. "See the tire? Go tire!" Make sure he commits to the tire before you release his collar.
4. Raise the height only an inch or two at a time.

> The major mistake with the tire jump is raising the height too quickly. The tire is a difficult obstacle that requires absolute precision, especially for larger dogs who just barely fit through the opening. You must go slowly with this obstacle.

If you rush your dog by raising the height too quickly, he will hesitate at some crucial point, doubting his ability to "hit the bulls-eye" that high up. If he loses his nerve at the last second, he will take the easy route by ducking under the tire or squeezing between the tire and the frame—and you will have pushed him into a bad habit that might be difficult to break.

So go slowly. Raise the height only an inch at a time, and work on that height for several sessions before raising it another inch or two.

5. Now, once you have the tire at full height, leave it there.

Yes, this is different advice than I've given for other obstacles! Usually I recommend keeping obstacles low so you don't put stress on your dog's bones and joints.

The tire jump is different. The tire jump requires such precision that once your dog has learned how to launch himself through the circle at a particular height, he needs regular practice at that same, consistent height so he doesn't forget where the bull's-eye is, so to speak.

Of course, if he's not going to compete in agility, simply choose a low height that will be easier on his bones and joints—and set it there all the time.

The tire jump requires physical and mental coordination that **puppies** should not be asked for. It's too risky when their body is still developing. If you're going to do the tire jump with a puppy, set it at only a couple of inches off the ground.

Teeter-totter

Word #100: "Go Teeter"

The teeter-totter (seesaw) is another tough obstacle. The teeter is a single plank ten inches wide and twelve feet long. Like a children's seesaw, it's set on a hinged support so it goes up and down at either end. It's only two feet off the ground, so this not a high obstacle—its difficulty is in its movement, which most dogs find unsettling.

To negotiate the teeter, your dog walks up the plank to the **pivot point** (tipping point) near the center of the board. Then he creeps forward until his weight tips the other end of the plank down so he can walk down to the bottom. Like the dogwalk and A-frame, the teeter has contact zones at each end of the plank that must be touched.

> To keep the teeter from banging and startling your dog as it hits the ground, attach a strip of foam or rubber to each end of the plank, along the bottom edge.

You'll need helpers

You will need at least one helper to teach this obstacle—preferably two.

- One helper stands on one side of your dog to prevent him from jumping off the side of the teeter when it starts to move.
- You stand on the other side of your dog, holding his collar.
- Your second helper holds the far end of the teeter firmly in the air so the ramp won't move when your dog makes his first trip up the incline. You don't want to scare him on his first trip!

Teaching the teeter

1. Lead your dog by the collar up the ramp. When you reach the pivot point, STOP and give him a treat around the center of the plank where his weight would normally begin to tip the board down.

   The pivot point is different for each dog. The smaller the dog, the farther past center he will need to go before his weight is enough to begin tipping the board.

2. As he chews his treat, your helper should slowly lower the far end of the teeter to the ground. (Your other helper should be ready to steady your dog in case he tries to leap off when the board begins to move.) Hopefully, eating the treat will hold your dog's attention so that he hardly notices the board moving.

3. Once the ramp is resting firmly on the ground, walk your dog calmly down and off the ramp.

> Repeat this simple, confidence-building walk-over many times. Don't use any commands other than encouraging words. For many dogs, the teeter is the obstacle that becomes their nemesis because they have a scary initial experience. So take this obstacle slowly and don't attach its name yet.

4. When your dog is comfortable walking up the ramp to the pivot point and eating his treat, begin adding the phrase, "TIP it!" to cue your dog that the plank will begin to move at this particular point.

5. Eventually it will be time for your dog to start tipping the board himself. Have him take one step past the pivot point as your helper lowers the ramp only a little bit—as though your dog's step had actually pushed it down that far. Stop right at that point and give your dog a treat for his successful step.

Now have him take another step—accompanied by another slight lowering of the board—and accompanied by another treat. Step by step, your dog should come down the ramp with your helper guiding the end of the teeter so it doesn't come down too fast.

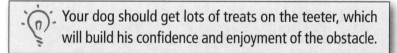

Your dog should get lots of treats on the teeter, which will build his confidence and enjoyment of the obstacle.

You still have work to do on this obstacle and I recommend getting help from a dedicated Dog Agility book, because this can be a tricky obstacle. But soon you will be able to progress to a walk-by and then a run-by. That's when you start attaching the phrase "Go teeter!"

A beginner's teeter—good for puppies, too

For puppies (and sensitive adult dogs who are intimidated by the big teeter), you can build a beginner's teeter. Instead of a plank set two feet off the ground and a pivot point that tips the teeter sharply, you place the plank about six inches off the ground, resting atop a wooden sphere that's been cut in half. This rounded fulcrum gently rocks the teeter toward the ground.

You can also place a three-foot-square piece of plywood atop a tennis ball. Play with your puppy on this moving platform by luring him on and off with treats. His confidence will build as he discovers that the rocking board is fun and harmless!

Everyday obstacles—use it or lose it!

The world is filled with obstacles for your dog. Look around for them. A large boulder he can jump onto. A fallen log he can walk across. Playground equipment at the park. Neighborhood kids on their hands and knees, bunched up next to each other, arching their backs and forming a human "tunnel" your small dog can run through!

Show your dog how to traverse:

- stairs (including those with open risers)
- a narrow foot bridge
- railroad tracks
- manhole covers
- vinyl and tile floors

I've seen dogs walking along the sidewalk suddenly bolt sideways because their foot touched a metal manhole cover. Some dogs raised on wall-to-wall carpeting don't know how to walk on slippery vinyl. A Doberman I knew refused to walk across a wooden or tile floor because he didn't like the clicking sound his toenails made.

Then there was the young Rottweiler arriving at his first agility trial. He was clearly happy to be there, ready to show off his abilities to "Jump!" and "Climb it!" and "Walk it!" Except that he balked at walking up the half-dozen stairs leading to the exhibition floor! His frustrated owner spent the next ten minutes trying to coax her 120-pound dog upstairs. "He's never seen stairs before," she admitted sheepishly.

The little things we forget to teach!

Get your dog out into the world. He needs lots of experiences so he learns to trust that anything you ask him to do is possible and safe.

Seeing the world stimulates his brain, as well as his body. A stimulated brain develops new connections between brain cells, and dogs with lots of connections between brain cells think more quickly—they actually become smarter and more capable of figuring things out. And a stimulated brain has a greater ability to grow new cells, which is especially reassuring as your dog ages.

> ☼ So help your dog develop a healthy brain. Take him out into the world and let him PRACTICE the vocabulary words you're teaching him!

Challenging activities your dog can participate in

Thirty minutes of participating in a mentally challenging activity will make your dog happier (and smarter) than a boring two-hour walk. Dogs love mental exercise!

- Agility
- Carting
- Earthdog
- Flyball
- Frisbee®
- Herding
- Hunting trials
- Lure coursing
- Musical freestyle (doggy dancing)
- Rally-O
- Schutzhund/Ringsport
- Scootering/Skijoring
- Tracking
- Weight pulling

Find out about these sports by Googling them on the Internet. You might start at *http://en.wikipedia.org/wiki/Dog_sports*.

> ☼ Dogs who participate in challenging activities become smarter, happier, more confident, and better-behaved. Help your dog be the best he can be. Have fun with him!

Chapter 20

Dog Care Wisdom: 11 Things You Must Do Right To Keep Your Dog Healthy and Happy

You might think you already know how to raise your dog—what to feed him, when to get his shots, when to have him spayed or neutered, how to prevent fleas, how to recognize symptoms of health problems, and so on.

The problem is….

> **When it comes to raising your dog, most of what you've read or been told to do is based on**
>
> **OUTDATED MISINFORMATION.**

For example, you may have read or been told…

- That you should feed your dog a premium dog food like Science Diet or Iams.
- That you should feed your dog kibble because it's good for his teeth.
- That your puppy needs three or four shots for distemper, parvovirus, coronavirus, leptospirosis, and kennel cough.
- That your adult dog needs annual booster shots.
- That your dog needs to be wormed regularly.
- That you should control fleas with a flea collar.
- That you should neuter your dog at six months old.
- That you should choose a vet based on how friendly he is, or how happy your dog is to see him, or how reasonable his fees are.

ALL OF THIS IS INCORRECT.

That's why I wrote **Dog Care Wisdom: 11 Things You Must Do Right To Keep Your Dog Healthy and Happy**.

- To tell you WHICH THINGS you've read about or heard about, when it comes to raising your dog, that are *outdated misinformation*.
- And to give you the RIGHT information about raising your dog the RIGHT way, an 11-Step Health Care Program that will keep your dog healthy and happy for a lifetime.

In *Dog Care Wisdom*

- You'll learn how to feed your dog. I'll recommend the best foods—and tell you which foods are the worst.
- You'll learn that vaccination requirements have changed drastically—for example, your dog no longer needs annual booster shots. Most vets won't tell you this because they make money giving vaccinations. I'll tell you which vaccinations your dog really needs and which ones are a waste of money—or harmful.
- You'll learn how to keep fleas and ticks off your dog—I'll even name all the products you shouldn't use.
- You'll learn how to keep your dog safe. I'll tell you about 25 safety hazards in your home and yard, and 20 things that are probably in your house right now that can cause itchy skin and allergies in dogs.
- You'll learn how to groom your dog—how to bathe him, clean his eyes, ears, and teeth, clip his nails, and trim or clip his coat.
- I'll tell you how to decide whether you should breed your dog, the advantages and disadvantages of neutering, how old your dog should be for neutering—and why neutering at the wrong age is a big mistake.
- You'll learn how to find the right vet. All the effort you've put into keeping your dog healthy can be undone in the blink of an eye by the wrong vet. I'll tell you exactly what questions you should ask your vet to determine whether he's any good.

> Good health over a lifetime doesn't just happen by luck. What you do NOW will affect your dog's health for years to come.

When you follow the complete health care program in **Dog Care Wisdom**, you will be doing everything you can for your dog to live a healthier, happier, longer life. You'll avoid unnecessary vet expenses, too! **Honest. You will.**

To purchase **Dog Care Wisdom: 11 Things You Must Do Right To Keep Your Dog Healthy and Happy,** visit my website at *www.yourpurebredpuppy.com.*

Index